Next to the Ice shows that "The friends and families made in hockey are ~~~~~~~~ Next to the ice ~~~~~~~ nadian athlete's life i ~~~~~~

- Cassie~~~~~~~~~~~~~~~~~~~~~~~~~~~~~~~~~~~ commentator and Cap~~~~~ ~~ ~ ~~~~~~~ ~~~~ ~~~~~~ ~~~~~~~ ~eams

"The key foundation for success and development for any hockey player is through their local hockey association via Hockey Canada and most importantly their family."

- Dr. Ken Gagner, DC, SCMC, BSc, BEd, CK, BHK, HP1 certified hockey coach

"I did not realize how lucky I was to grow up in small-town hockey with such a group of dedicated and talented teammates and coaches. Having a great minor hockey experience 'next to the ice' makes all the difference for players."

- Todd Warriner, CHL commentator and former NHL forward

"Fans like the ones in *Next to the Ice* have such a positive impact on players and teams. The atmosphere while playing at home with cheering fans can give you that extra boost on the ice, making the difference between winning and losing."

- Defenseman T.J. Brodie, #7 Calgary Flames

NEXT
TO THE
ICE

Library and Archives Canada C 796. **'ublication**

Cobb, Cam, author
    Next to the ice : exploring the cult 962 0971 of hockey in Canada
/ Cam Cobb, Christopher J. Greig, Kar<
Issued in print and electronic formats. COB
ISBN 978-1-77161-186-2 (paperback).-- 187-9 (html).--
ISBN 978-1-77161-188-6 (pdf)

    1. Hockey--Canada. 2. Hockey--Social aspects--Canada. I. Greig,
Christopher J. (Christopher John), 1965-, author II. Smith, Kara, 1967-,
author

    III. Title.
GV848.4.C3C62 2016   796.9620971   C2016-904344-4
                                                  C2016-904345-2

Published by Mosaic Press, Oakville, Ontario, Canada, 2016.

MOSAIC PRESS, Publishers

Printed and Bound in Canada

Designed by Courtney Blok

ONTARIO ARTS COUNCIL
CONSEIL DES ARTS DE L'ONTARIO
an Ontario government agency
un organisme du gouvernement de l'Ontario

We acknowledge the Ontario Arts Council
for their support of our publishing program

We acknowledge the Ontario Media Development Corporation
for their support of our publishing program

Funded by the   Financé par le
Government   gouvernement   **Canada**
of Canada   du Canada

MOSAIC PRESS
1252 Speers Road, Units 1 & 2
Oakville, Ontario L6L 5N9
phone: (905) 825-2130

info@mosaic-press.com

www.mosaic-press.ca

NEXT
TO THE
ICE

BY CAM COBB,
CHRISTOPHER J. GREIG
AND KARA SMITH

 mosaicPRESS

CONTENTS

INTRODUCTION

*N*ext to the Ice: Exploring the Culture and Community of Hockey in Canada is a collection of personal and formal essays on a topic that
matters to many Canadians: ice hockey. Hockey is not only one of Canada's national sports, but is a deeply ingrained thread that has been
interlaced and woven into the very cultural, social and economic fab-
ric of Canadian society. In this anthology, then, we are interested in
exploring much more closely the thread, in its rich texture, in order
to bring to light some of the uniquely Canadian places and spaces,
contemporary and historical, and the real and imagined in relation to
Canada's hockey communities and culture. The essays in this book not
only showcase various features of hockey communities and culture, but
also provide a meditation and an analysis on the meaning of hockey to
those close to the ice.

In Chapter One, entitled "Understanding Hockey Cosmology," Cam
surveys the literature on the birth of professional hockey in Canada.
And in doing this, he explores the way our ever-shifting sense of hockey history links to our fluid notion of history itself. The way we understand ourselves in the present is, in part, reflected in the way we
portray ourselves in the past. And this is true for pro hockey as it is

for any other aspect of Canadian history. As such, this chapter brings a new way of looking at hockey history. Hockey is a big business. History itself, as a long-standing subject of debate and fascination, is eternal. Given these realities, writing about hockey's past, as we might expect, is a virtual cottage industry—and has been for quite some time. Yet for some reason the origins and early years of the NHL have received sporadic attention since the league's tumultuous birth in 1917. Over the decades, hockey chroniclers have focused their pens (or keyboards) on mercurial personalities, telling yarns about franchise dramas and great quests for the Stanley Cup. Yet there remain gaps in our knowledge of the pre and early NHL eras. Of course, the upcoming one-hundredth anniversary of the NHL has prompted some historians – including Canada's last Prime Minister – to throw their proverbial hats into the history ring, contributing to a new (or, at the very least, newly told) origin story, or cosmology. But the question remains: If we are rewriting our history, what does this say about us today?

In Chapter Six, entitled "All this Useless Junk," Cam examines literature on the phenomenon of collecting, as well as the hockey memorabilia market itself—and in doing so puts forward three reasons that explain what drives so many people, mostly male Canadians, to collect hockey memorabilia. And in developing this chapter, Cam learned much about the psychology and nationalist dimensions of the ever-growing hockey memorabilia market. North America's sports merchandise business exceeds $12 billion every year. It is vast—and, like the universe, it is expanding. Hockey collecting – as well as the production, buying, and selling of hockey memorabilia – marks a healthy slice of that robust industry. For a variety of reasons, hockey enthusiasts find themselves ensnared by the pursuit of different hockey-related items, including trading cards, ticket stubs, game programs, game-used equipment, arena relics, team jerseys, collectible coins, and many other such goodies. Yet what compels these hobbyists to seek out and gather these various objects of memorabilia? And what is it about hockey in particular that is special in Canada's sports collecting landscape? In a personal narrative and discussion, three key aspects of hockey collecting are explored in this chapter, namely: community, nostalgia, and the thrill of the hunt and satisfaction of ownership.

Christopher's work explores how social class functioned in the 1970s to create the material conditions whereby some men saw hockey, in particular as a hockey enforcer, as the only way out of a hardscrabble life. Some working-class boys grew up knowing really one thing, that it was either going to be a life in the coal-mines or scraping by on the farm, or, fighting their way up the ranks of junior hockey into the pros for something of a better life. For these boys, it meant fighting battles against others boys, beyond endurance, beyond cracked ribs, ruptured kidneys and repeated blows to the head. Instead of running from the pain and the violence, these working class boys stepped into it. Clearly, as you will read, some wounds were too deep or were too close to the bone, and no matter how hard they tried, they just could not stop the internal bleeding. In the end, some of these men seemed to have risked everything, because they really had nothing.

Christopher's meditation on hockey communities and culture in Canada also takes into careful consideration the way boys' organized hockey today remains a pivotal part in the socialization of young boys. In this, he sees boys' organized hockey as a central place and space for the production of a particular model of masculinity that, to some measure or another, is deeply problematic in developing healthy young men. This world is a hyper-masculine world, largely empty of women, and its hopes and fantasies and stratagems are often grounded in patriarchal practices. Christopher's meditation on hockey communities and cultures asks a central question that is often unasked-what do boys really learn playing organized hockey?

Who is 'next to the ice' as much as players and fans? The parents and family members of hockey players. Kara's chapters explore the positive side of developing Canada's elite hockey athletes, the world inside of hockey families, parents and friends found at practices and games and tournaments all over North America. Hockey, like football or lacrosse, receives sensational press for its male-dominated aggression and players' injuries, but the story less-often-told is that of the thrill and benefit of hard work, team bonding, and realizing what skill the human body is capable of! To develop an elite athlete, on ice, the entire family is committed to practice schedules, driving, camps, tournaments and travel. And the elite athlete is in a continual process of discovering what s/he loves on the ice. Some love the feel of the speed of their skates off the bench, across the ice and into the corner. Other players love the connection the puck makes from one stick to another. Some like the creative, crazy, sticky situations made to deke your way through the labyrinth of ice, sticks, pucks and defenders to the goal. Finding, and developing, that one love in the game is how families and parents support our national athletes. That ever-changing character of hockey players is what keeps fans and those next to the ice fascinated by what will happen next. If you have never felt the love of sport at this level, these chapters will enable you to experience the thrill and mystery of one of Canada's favourite pastimes for yourself, from the inside.

Most book introductions provide a series of chapter-by-chapter summaries—telling the reader what's ahead in a forward-moving chronological sequence. In this sense, they foreshadow and inform readers as to what will be discussed in the book. While we intend to achieve the same end in this introduction, we have approached the task in a slightly different way. We will speak to our own chapters and involvement in the project using a short reflection. Cam begins this process by speaking to Chapters One and Six, followed by Christopher, speaking indirectly to the motivations that fuelled the writing of Chapters Two and Four, and finally Kara who sheds some light on the origins of Chapters Three and Five. Our chapters are not separate from one another—and in many ways overlap, interconnect and, when placed side-by-side form a whole. Perhaps the coming together of different ideas and approaches to hockey to form a whole is simply a natural outcome of our collaborative process.

Cam

Over a period of nearly two years I have thought a lot about my own experiences with hockey, as well as the sport's august position in Canadian culture. It has been a long road of contemplating the game, revisiting moments of the past, and encountering feelings of nostalgia. Casting my mind back to the 1970s, I cannot recall the first time I was captivated by a game, the earliest time I skated at a rink, or opening my first pack of O-Pee-Chee hockey cards. These are three things that, from the vantage point of today, seem to have always been a part of my life. There was always NHL hockey at Maple Leaf Gardens (though ticket prices meant it was visited scarcely), there was always outdoor rinks at Trace Manes Park, and there were always those little cardboard relics of the NHLs finest superstars, near-superstars, and mediocrities. These three things – NHL games, rinks, and collectibles (a trinity of sorts) – were always a part of my life. *Weren't they?*

While I know this isn't true, my consciousness says otherwise. Like my parents, my first childhood home near Victoria Park and Danforth Avenue in Toronto, and my parents' 1969 racing green Dodge Dart convertible, hockey seems to always have been a part of my formative years. Hockey was and is a permanent fixture in my life, a natural part of the landscape. Yet on a deeper level, I know that hockey was not always a part of my life. There was a time when it was not a part of my interests, habits, routines and schema. Although I do not know precisely when hockey seeped into my consciousness, it has remained in my mind for decades. Although I no longer play hockey, I still watch games now and then. And while hockey collecting is no longer a part of my habits and routines, I cannot see myself ever letting go of my collection of hockey memorabilia, such as cards, books and game programs. In all honesty, I expect my daughters to cherish my hockey memorabilia in the not so distant future. Perhaps this is wishful thinking.

When sketching out this book, we agreed that I would take on a chapter on history and another on collecting. Yet I was not yet sure what exactly I would write about these two aspects of the sport. Over time, I thought about what intrigued me about hockey as well as what has kept me connected (albeit tenuously) to the sport. As I already mentioned, I haven't played the game in decades. Why can't I bring myself to get rid of my hockey memorabilia? Why do I imagine my two daughters will treasure my old hockey artefacts in the future? My answers to these questions motivated me—and in part, guided me as I crafted my two chapters.

Christopher

Many of my childhood memories are of hockey. These memories exert an influence on me in a way others do not by the feeling of childhood pleasure, freedom and innocence they invoke. To be sure, looking back on my childhood years the prominence of hockey culture shaped and provided the contours of my boyhood: Oakridge Arena, an old cold barn of a rink, wooden Victoriaville hockey sticks with the straight blades, Bauer skates with the heavy cold steel blades, pucks, outdoor rinks, boyhood friends, orange road hockey balls, curved plastic stick blades, and replica Boston Bruin jerseys; these are some of the 'stuff' that filled my early years. Not surprisingly, they remain in one way or another in orbit, real or imagined, gravitationally bound to the structure of my memories.

My memories of hockey and childhood are also connected to my father. It was my father, Ted, whom I remember mostly driving me back and forth to the local hockey rink for games and practices. The 6:30am practices during the week would have been a form of drudgery for him I am sure, something that I did not understand as a child, but do now. Children often take for granted what parents do for them. As a boy, I certainly took for granted what my mother, Vera and father, Ted did for me. My father once took my brother and I to watch Bobby Orr and the rest of the Boston Bruins in training camp in the old Treasure Island hockey rink, located off Wellington Road in London, Ontario in the early 1970s. That excursion remains a vivid memory. But there are many smaller but tangible connections between my father, my childhood and hockey than this.

As a child, I remember waking up early and going to the kitchen to see whether or not my father brought home a package of O-Pee-Chee hockey cards. He sometimes left a pack on the kitchen table or on top of the refrigerator in our house on Longbow Road in London. He must have done that numerous times, as I accumulated a modest collection of hockey cards over time. And, I had my favorite hockey cards. To this day, the 1971-1972 O-Pee-Chee Ken Dryden rookie card stands out in my mind; his body coiled in a deep low crouch poised for an imaginary shot, his blocker with a few strands of white tap around it grips his stick, his glove hand almost reaching down to his skate, all of which was set against an orange background, situated in an oval border. The cards I would sometimes take into my room and between the dark and the daylight, before I had to get ready for school, I would sift and sort through them. It was a simple childhood pleasure. In the early 1970s, like many fathers, my father was also responsible for building a backyard hockey rink. This time at our new house on Havenridge Crescent, London. It was in the winter of 1975 or maybe 1976, and I remember my dad as he stood in the cold darkness of a winter's night, flooding the rink with an everyday green garden hose. My brother Mark and I would spend hours on our backyard rink, skating over bumpy, uneven ice and shooting pucks into the snow banks, or sometimes over them. When the puck did go over the snow bank becoming buried, we would scramble over the bank with our skates on, through the snow to retrieve it. On nights like these, the cold of the winter's evening numbed our noses and ears, sometimes our feet. But we did not care. We were on the ice.

As a boy, life was mostly about the ice, about hockey, the game gave my boyhood a deep dimension. I loved the low winter light, especially the way it illuminated the uneven ice in our backyard, or, on our street where my friends and I would play endless games of road hockey. The cold winter's light, the snow and the cold, the feeling of elation while chasing a ball or a puck, frame my earliest and fondest impressions of my childhood. But my boyhood was also marked by major hockey-related events. I remember very clearly, for instance, my Grade 2 class at St. Thomas More School in London, Ontario, in September of 1972, huddled around one of the school's black and white TV sets mounted on an AV cart to watch one of the televised games between Canada and the Soviet Union. The Summit Series, as it was billed, loomed large over parts of my childhood, as it still does over our national mythology. Without a doubt, the Series is a key cultural and historical marker in Canada. Paul Henderson's series winning goal, now so closely tied to a sense of Canadian identity also remains connected to my youth. But these memories and experiences I now know are not so simple. The way I remember the past is a complicated process, which is to say memory work is tricky. To be sure, childhood in general, is a complicated time, not the least of which is how it is powerfully influenced by broader forces and social structures, not readily visible to a young boy's eye, or, an older man's memory.

My childhood was gendered, an idea that began to crystalize over time along the margins of my own consciousness. I did not see as a child the way in which my childhood world in general, hockey in particular was so rigidly structured along gender lines. I never once thought that the reason my brother and I both played organized ice hockey and my sister Susan didn't, had anything to do with systems of gender oppression and sexism. Like many people of the time, I just thought that was the way it was. I certainly did not know when I was five or six years of age, that hockey was a key site for the socialization of Canadian boys, a key site for the production of an 'appropriate' boyhood. No boy I knew thought that. No parents, including my own, viewed organized hockey as the site for the making of men and masculinity situated in the context of a gendered, capitalist society. All I knew was that I loved to play, and play I did, day in and day out, all winter long. Certainly, as a product of the 1970s, where the linkage between hockey and appropriate boyhood was thought to be so natural was there any serious consideration that a boy should not play hockey. It was simply expected of a boy. It was viewed ideologically and otherwise as simply a natural rite of passage for any Canadian boy, and to reject hockey's invitation to play, put you outside the circle of a so-called 'real' boyhood. As a child (and as an adult) you are simply unaware of how ideological structures shape and influence your life; you believe as I did that you are making particular choices out of your own complete free will. As an adult I now know that why we choose to engage in the activities we do as children, is far more complicated that initially thought. I now see ice hockey as an organized sport and institution structured within the confines and contours of a capitalist gendered society. Its purpose, to some degree or another, was and is to socialize boys in its own interest and to produce particular kinds of boys, and now girls, and not others. Although I have fond memories of my hockey playing experiences and I remain engaged with the game as a father of a 15 year old young woman (Jaden) who continues to play competitive hockey since beginning at age 5, and as the head coach of my youngest daughter's (Emma) Windsor Wildcats' Bantam A team and also as a recreational player for over 30 years and still plays three times a week, I now see it in a far more complicated way. Though as for that, this is true, I think, of all things, not just hockey.

The two chapters I have penned originate out of my early boyhood experiences, as understood and interpreted across the span of 50 years or so. I little knew then how much a hold those intense experiences and now memories have had on me, all those cold winter nights so many years ago, next to the ice.

Kara

In the middle ages, those that were fast runners or strong or good athletes would work their way up the social chain towards a warrior or knight in the king's army. Today, in Canada, we have hockey. Although

I was a national athlete myself, I am a woman, and as such, have always been skeptical of male dominated sports, especially ones with such seemingly violent stories. Although I did grow up in a family of men, and now live in a household of men, I did not grow up in a 'hockey family.' Hockey was too expensive for a first generation immigrant family like ours, so we played 'school sports' like volleyball and basketball that, at the time, were free. My husband, on the other hand, did come from a hockey family and when our sons wanted to begin playing, our first year of hockey was an initiation into a world that was new to both myself and my children.

I have always been fascinated by other 'cultures' and the interpersonal systems within the culture, the 'ethnography' of my surroundings. Hockey truly is a culture unto Canada, and it is fascinating. Hockey has received some interesting criticisms: "It's a sport for goons." "It's only played in countries with ice." "It's a minority sport." But hockey is also known as a sport that grew out of the 'great white north,' it is an outdoor sport, a winter sport – fresh and clean. It is uniquely Northern.

At first, I could not understand Canadians' fascination with hockey. *'Why are they so attached to the outcome of a six-year-old's practice?'* But I also knew that, being an athlete myself, commitment to a team, practice, and daily personal development is character building. It forms confidence. It builds relationships. You learn how to trust partners in very difficult situations. You learn how to push yourself to an edge and see where you come out.

Chapter Five, "Ice," explores the ethnography inside a typical small-town hockey environment for parents. It describes the conversations and thoughts of the parents of elite hockey players. What do people say to children who, like gifted students, are bound for physical feats of greatness? What is the home life like in the week of a household of hockey players? How do they best learn? How do their minds focus and their bodies endure? This chapter explores that obsession of a discipline, and what it is like to be a part of that 24-7 work-play life. If you want to know about Canadians and hockey, and 'why the addiction?', then you have bought the right book.

"The Yellow Brick Road," Chapter Three, really evolved out of the rink community I was a part of. As I was learning about hockey systems and players and parents, I began to notice that at least once a year, all teams feel they need to have a 'fun game' out on a canal or lake or pond. Why? Also, in the National Hockey League (NHL) each year, there is a 'Winter Classic,' a game with two NHL teams that takes place outdoors every January 1st. Tickets for the 'Winter Classic' sell out as soon as they are released. Sales reach mythical proportions; higher than a rock concert. Why? Any, or most, hockey games we have ever played were indoors on a hockey rink, not outside. Why outside? *'It must be historic,'* I thought. The more I read, the more I realized there were two or three key pieces of Canadian Literature that every single Canadian had either read, or was very familiar with, and those books were about hockey being played outside on a pond. The start of the formal game in Canada also began outdoors, or at least was promoted outdoors by no less than the Queen's representative himself. This image of 'what hockey should be' presents some interesting duplicities in the public perception of the players themselves, and "The Yellow Brick Road" metaphor describes this incongruity.

Next to the Ice is an intriguing and unique exploration into hockey communities and culture in Canada. With a mixture of six formal and personal essays on timely themes, the book provides readers with keen insights into various key areas of elite and professional hockey including fan culture, franchise drama, the rise of the hockey enforcer, hockey's gender politics, and the complicated off-ice micro-politics so often found in hockey parent communities. *Next to the Ice* is unique as it is the work of three university educators and researchers, who are also hockey-parents and ex-players. In crafting this book, we bring the reader inside the world of 'rink rats,' hockey families, and hardcore fans and collectors that dot hockey's cultural and social landscape. Now, we invite you to turn the page and join us on our journey, delving into hockey culture and community in Canada—a culture and community that are both inclusive and exclusive, old and new, real and imagined.

CHAPTER ONE:
Understanding Hockey Cosmology

In this chapter, I explore the cosmology of professional hockey. A combination of the Greek words "kosmos" and "ology," cosmology is the study of the origin, development, and fate of the universe.[1] The first of these three components to a cosmology is rooted in a culture's origin stories. Origin stories, according to anthropologist Mari Womack, "are symbolic stories describing how the universe and its inhabitants came to be."[2] Similarly, I am concerned with the symbolic origin stories that served to provide the foundation for the ongoing formation of a hockey cosmology.

While different origin stories may gain widespread acceptance and endure for a time, they may also be modified, expanded, elaborated on, but they also may disappear—and as such, cosmology is fluid, sometimes contested, but always in flux.[3] Astronomy and physics researcher Marc Davis notes that while scientific cosmologies sometimes develop slowly, key moments of raised awareness lead to "critical leap[s] in cosmological understanding."[4]

---

1 Stephen Battersby, "Introduction: Cosmology," New Scientist, September 4 2006. Accessed November 1 2015 https://www.newscientist.com/article/dn9988-introduction-cosmology/.
2 Mari Womack, *Symbols and Meaning: A Concise Introduction* (Toronto, ON: AltaMira Press, a division of Rowman & Littlefield Publishers Inc., 2005), 81.
3 Marc Davis, "The Modern Creation Myth," *Bulletin of the American Academy of Arts and Sciences*, 45:8 (1992), 47-64.
4 Ibid, 57.

This is also true of the cosmology of professional hockey. At certain historical junctures, the prevailing and popular and mostly conservative cosmology of hockey has been punctured and forced to expand by newly generated narratives that incorporate identities and voices that were erased in the original origin stories. As such, the complicated and complex process in the ongoing formation of a hockey cosmology, like any other, is ever shifting.

More specifically, I focus on the cosmology of hockey's thorny genesis—or how popular hockey historians have created an origin story, and then reshaped it over the years. I will begin by surveying a variety of works of history—ones that focus on the origin and growth of professional hockey and the National Hockey League (NHL) in the first three decades of the twentieth century. Following this, I will discuss a recently published hockey history. To this end, I will address such questions as: How has the birth of pro hockey (and the NHL) been portrayed by popular writers and historians? When it comes to the formation of a hockey cosmology, what is and is not discussed in these chronicles? In order to engage with these various histories, I have divided this chapter into the following three segments: (1) Traditional Cosmology, (2) Alternative Cosmology, and (3) One More History. With this subject matter in mind, we turn our attention to the mythmaking and myth breaking found in popular histories about hockey in Canada.

Traditional Cosmology – The Great Man Theory of Hockey History

Popular histories about hockey have become increasingly common, filling bookstore and library shelves. Despite the growth of the genre, hockey histories tend to be very similar in that they draw from a Great Man theory. The so-called Great Man theory of history emerged out of the work of Thomas Carlyle in the nineteenth century where he stated that history can largely be explained by the powerful influence of 'great men.'[5] Great men, or heroes, were thought to be particular individuals who have power

---

[5] See Robert L. Carneiro, "Herbert Spencer as an Anthropologist." *The Journal of Libertarian Studies*, 5:2 (1981): 153-210.

and influence due to their intelligence, skill, charisma, or whatever—in a way that they had significant impact on historical events. To put it slightly differently, a hero or a Great Man theory of history explains all historical events as an outcome individual decisions made by individual men.

The Great Man theory of history profoundly shaped the formation of the cosmology of professional hockey in its early days. The connection between the Great Man theory of history and the creation of an early cosmology of professional hockey is visible in four variations of the traditional hockey history narrative. These four broad categories are as follows: *(1) The Hero's Biography, (2) Storied Franchises and Enterprising Men, (3) The Quest for the Cup, and (4) The Great Saga.* While many traditional narratives fall into one of these four general categories, some straddle two, or even more. No matter which category a hockey history falls into, each one in their own way functions at some level to fuel the notion that the history of professional hockey has been powerfully shaped by individual struggles, trials and tribulations, and the overcoming of obstacles and great odds in the quest for hockey greatness. As such, the Great Man theory of history that has underpinned the early and ongoing formation of the prevailing cosmology of professional hockey has been recycled time and time again through popular hockey chronicles. It is to this theory and myth that I turn my attention to now.

The Hero's Biography

Knowingly or not, numerous hockey historians have employed the Great Man theory to explain the hockey world through the hero's biography. Many of their works focus on famous personalities, such as star players and notorious owners from the sport's early years. In recounting the exploits of these figures, writers have fixed their attention on their heroic life journeys, namely the lone great man and his great feats and trials and tribulations.

Although hockey biographies are plentiful today they were not the first books published on the sport. While instructional books dominated the hockey publishing market from the late 1800s to the early 1900s, hockey biographies started to appear in the 1940s.[6] An early such work is the 1949 collection, *Hockey Heroes: Canadian Sports Album.* Written by Canadian sportswriter Ron McAllister, the book presents short sketches of famous players harkening from the first three decades of the NHL. In addition to drawing from his friendships with newspaper writers and broadcasters, McAllister drew from a well of first-hand accounts to paint vignettes of historic stars, including Irvine Wallace 'Ace' Bailey and Francis Michael 'King' Clancy.

While he was born in 1917, the very year the NHL was formed, McAllister benefitted from gathering stories from those who were directly involved in the League's earliest era. In his Introduction, he thanks goaltender George Hainsworth, for instance, "for bringing to light many forgotten details of his own great goalkeeping feats in the earlier days of the game."[7] Here, we see a high value placed on first-hand accounts along with uncovering "forgotten" moments. Ron McAllister would repeat this process with two additional books released in the early 1950s. While McAllister retold the stories of various 'stars' from the past, his narrative was limited, as it focused on a select few heroic men—all of whom were players who, for lack of a better word, were seen and treated by fans and owners as chattel.

A key problem that comes out of the early formation of a hockey cosmology that relies on stories upon stories about individuals who powerfully and decisively impacted the sport's course of events is that it fails to take into account the historical context. For instance, the conservative hockey cosmology in its early formation did little to connect the emergent foundation of professional hockey with a budding capitalist economy. So, the foundation of professional hockey needs to be understood from the perspective of capitalist entrepreneurs who saw in organized professional sport an opportunity for profit. The owners of professional

---

6 Carl Spandoni, "Hockey Books and Canadian Culture," *Historical Perspectives on Canadian Publishing.* Accessed November 1 2015 http://hpcanpub.mcmaster.ca/case-study/hockey-books-and-canadian-culture.

7 Ron McAllister, *Hockey Heroes: Canadian Sports Album* (Toronto, ON: McClelland & Stewart Limited, 1949), x. McAllister went on to pen two additional collections of vignettes over the following few years entitled *Hockey Stars ... Today and Yesterday* (Toronto, ON: McClelland & Stewart Limited, 1950) and *More Hockey Stories: From the Canadian Sports Album* (Toronto, ON: McClelland & Stewart, 1952).

hockey teams were far less likely to be interested in the tales of heroic men, except as a way to promote professional hockey teams to the masses, then they were interested in the sport as a commodity, a consumer good, that was to be bought and sold. The bottom line was simply good stories told about hockey's heroic men, sold tickets.

Nonetheless, using life stories to create an early hockey cosmology was a strategy writers used that cut across decades. While a smattering of biographies appeared in the 1950s and 1960s, they did not focus on the early days of pro hockey in Canada. Perhaps it was the NHL's fiftieth anniversary that sparked a renewed interest in its origins. On the other hand, perhaps it was the diminishing number of survivors from the distant past that compelled writers to seek out these aging icons and chronicle their stories. Perhaps it was a combination of the two. Whatever the cause, in the 1970s, broadcaster and journalist Eric Whitehead drew from contemporary newspaper accounts as well as conversations with aging players, to piece together the life stories of three prominent male figures in hockey history: Fred 'Cyclone' Taylor, and the Patrick brothers, Lester and Frank. Both seminal works, *Cyclone Taylor: A Hockey Legend* (1977) and *The Patricks: Hockey's Royal Family* (1980), detail the lives of these three iconic and inventive personalities. While 'Cyclone' Taylor was an early star player, the Patrick brothers were entrepreneurs, team owners, and dominant players who had a hand in rewriting the rulebook of professional hockey. In his foreword to *The Patricks*, Whitehead thanks Taylor, stating that he was "a priceless source of intimate material and firsthand accounts."[8]

Like McAllister three decades earlier, Whitehead's emphasis on personal testimony as a method to promote historical hockey figures once again produces a fairly conservative hockey cosmology, which does little to draw our attention to the broader social, political and economic forces that have shaped and reshaped hockey's history.

Fast forward to the 1990s. Stan and Shirley Fischler relay the voices of larger-than-life men from hockey's early days to continue to perpetuate

---

8 Eric Whitehead, *The Patricks: Hockey's Royal Family* (Toronto, ON: Doubleday Canada Limited, 1980), vi. Also see Eric Whitehead, *Cyclone Taylor: A Hockey Legend* (Toronto, ON: Doubleday Canada Limited, 1977).

the myth that it is great men who create history. In their 1994 book, *Heroes and History: Voices from the NHL's Past!*, the two recall from interviews to share the stories of twenty people—six hailing from the NHL's first twelve seasons.[9] In the Introduction, Stan Fischler states that in 1968: "I began a formal pursuit of the oral history project. During a trip to the Northwest, my wife, Shirley, and I arranged a series of interviews with legendary hockey characters. The quest to obtain these historic interviews took us to many diverse venues."[10]

As time marched on it became impossible to gather stories directly from hockey's heroes, or even witnesses from pro hockey's origins—and as such, player biographies became the product of researching secondary sources. Consequently, the nature of this personality-driven cosmology shifted. In the late 1990s, for instance, Paul Quarrington edited a collection of tales – fictionalized histories – mostly from the NHL's early days.[11] Published in 1996 and entitled *Original Six: True Stories from Hockey's Classic Era,* the book offers an eclectic assortment of sketches associated with legendary players, such as Chicago goalie Charlie Gardiner and Bruin bruiser Eddie Shore. In selecting writers for the project, Quarrington explains, "I intended to go for emotional rightness over historical expertise."[12] When outlining the project to contributor Trent Frayne and not without a little irony, for instance, the editor advised: "Write us a little fiction ... Just make sure it's true."[13]

Whether they draw from first-hand stories or secondary sources, these Great Man histories present a window into the past that privileges biography. They focus on the lived experiences, magnitude, and presence of key hockey personalities in the first few decades of the twentieth century. These stories, such as the ones found in Quarrington's *Original Six* (1996), are ones of mythical heroes and villains. And these hockey heroes are often portrayed as exemplifying extraordinary characteris-

---

9 Stan Fischler and Shirley Fischler, *Heroes and History: Voices from the NHL's Past!* (Toronto, ON: McGraw-Hill Ryerson, 1994).
10 Ibid., v.
11 Paul Quarrington. editor, *Original Six: True Stories from Hockey's Classic Era* (Toronto, ON: Reed Books Canada, 1996).
12 Ibid., 8.
13 Ibid., 9.

tics—where they sometimes uphold and other times challenge the culture, labour landscape and market economy of the times. An example of this mythmaking can be seen in ways in which 'Cyclone' Taylor is often represented as a brash, anti-establishment individual—with a penchant to jump from team-to-team and league-to-league, and sit-out entire seasons.[14]

While earlier Great Man narratives draw from the testimonies of aging heroes, more recent portraits draw from a reservoir of newspaper accounts and supplementary documents. Yet these testimonies were taken many decades after the events in question, and many older newspaper accounts were penned by beat reporters who had a vested interested in the stories they were reporting, and people on whom they were reporting.[15] Although their sources may differ, all of these books tend to fall in line with the well-known Thomas Carlyle-based mantra: *'History is the biographies of great men.'* In very general terms, this sort of a cosmology is one that places great value on (and indeed constructs) the lives of mythical heroes and villains who have contributed to the larger narrative of pro hockey. And some of these stories focus on the stories of different franchises—and the men of enterprise who ran them.

Storied Franchises and Enterprising Men: The 'Survival of the Fittest'

The second variation of the Great Man cosmology worth considering is one that places the narrative of the storied franchise – and, more specifically, rugged entrepreneurs – at its center. In this cluster of chronicles, the dawn of pro hockey is presented as a time of great drama, where 'great' moguls fought one another, and fought against the odds to survive. Those who tell the stories of hockey teams reveal a view of history, and the 'Great Man' narrative, that is rooted in 'survival of the fittest' forms of economics. These historians produce works that range from meticulously researched chronicles to briefer sketches. Either way,

---

14 See, for instance, Chris Goyens and Frank Orr with Allan Turowetz and Jean-Luc Duguay, *Blades on Ice: A Century of Professional Hockey* (Markham, ON: TPE Publishing, 2001), 33.
15 Morey Holzman and Joseph Nieforth, *Deceptions and Doublecross: How the NHL Conquered Hockey* (Toronto, ON: The Dundurn Group, 2002).

stories produced by these chroniclers relate the experiences of franchise owners, league executives, and 'star' players – all enterprising men – to capitalism, and change.

Some popular histories have focused on the Montréal Canadiens, hockey's oldest and perhaps most storied franchise. One such book, a lively narrative by Chrys Goyens and Allan Turowetz, is titled *Lions in Winter* (1994). This epic narrative tells the tale of the team's creation by industrialist J. Ambrose O'Brien – who ran multiple teams in the NHA – then winds through the team's fragile early years after being purchased by ex-wrestler and sports promoter George Kennedy. These were years of fluctuating attendance, early successes – including the 1916 and 1924 Stanley Cups – and lineups peppered with superstars of the day including Georges 'the Chicoutimi Cucumber' Vezina, 'Newsy' Lalonde, 'Phantom' Joe Malone, and 'Bad' Joe Hall. In the revised edition of *Lions in Winter* (1994), Goyens and Turoweitz sum up a franchise-, economic-oriented view of hockey history as follows: "How does a sports organization come to be perceived as a viable business arrangement? More significantly, how does a sports organization sustain its standards of excellence over time, while others remain unsuccessful or mired in mediocrity?"[16]

To read about the New York Rangers, one may turn to Frank Boucher's recollections of the ups and downs of the team's early days, entitled *When the Rangers Were Young*. Published in 1973, the book puts forward a personal account of times long since passed, presented with the support of sportswriter Trent Frayne. For Boucher, a team's narrative is not only one of economic survival, but also one of hardships and friendships. Casting his eyes back to all the players, coaches, and lineups he worked with, and all of the challenges he and his teammates endured; Boucher ponders, "I found myself thinking back over those long and eventful years of triumph and failure, great happiness and shredding disappointment,

---

16 Goyens and Turoweitz first published *Lions in Winter* in 1987. They updated the book following the Canadiens 1993 Stanley Cup victory. See Chrys Goyens and Allan Turoweitz, *Lions in Winter* (revised second edition) (Toronto, ON: McGraw-Hill Ryerson, 1994), 18.

unforgettable years in that crazy time when the Rangers were young."[17] Published a few years after the NHL's fiftieth anniversary, Boucher's work draws heavily upon personal memories, focusing on older teams that enjoyed good times and survived bad times. Like so many hockey histories that draw from testimony, his work relies on one's memory of events that occurred over a half century earlier.

Over the past three decades, accounts of various defunct teams have appeared on bookshelves. Shortly after the 1992 reformation of the Ottawa Senators, Joan Finnigan wrote her personal account of the final years of the original incarnation of the team, entitled *Old Scores, New Goals* (1994).[18] After all, she was the daughter of all-star forward Frank Finnigan, who played nine seasons with Ottawa in the 1920s and 1930s. Another book on the Senators appeared over a decade later written by former Society for International Hockey Research (SIHR) president, Paul Kitchen. In his tome, entitled *Win, Tie or Wrangle: The Inside Story of the Old Ottawa Senators*: 1883-1935 (2008), Kitchen offers a richly detailed narrative of the 52-year life of the original Senators team.[19]

Yet some of these team chronicles focus on short-lived franchises. 1990 saw the publication of scholar Frank Cosentino's portrayal of the fleeting two-season campaign of the Renfrew Creamery Kings, entitled *Renfrew Millionaires: The Valley Boys of 1910* (1990).[20] In Cosentino's eyes, the team's descent marks a key moment in hockey's early years—a time that saw such places as Dawson City and Kenora challenge for the Cup. "The Renfrew Millionaires," he states, "represent the end of an era in hockey history. The 1910 season was the last hurrah of that period; Renfrew was the last of the small towns to have embarked on a civic crusade to win the Stanley Cup."[21] 2005 saw the publication of *Hamilton's Hockey Tigers,* David and Sam Wesley's compact account of the five-season life

17 Frank Boucher with Trent Frayne, *When the Rangers Were Young* (New York, NY: Dodd, Mead & Company, 1973), 14.

18 Joan Finnigan, *Old Scores, New Goals: The Story of the Ottawa Senators* (Kingston, ON: Quarry Press, 1994).

19 Paul Kitchen, *Win, Tie, or Wrangle: The Inside Story of the Old Ottawa Senators* 1883-1935 (Newcastle, ON: Penumbria Press, 2008).

20 Frank Cosentino, *Renfrew Millionaires: The Valley Boys of Winter 1910* (Burnstown, ON: The General Store Publishing House Inc., 1990).

21 Ibid., 7.

and abrupt end of the Hamilton Tigers—the only NHL team to initiate a player strike.[22] In chronicling the Tigers' story, a narrative that is often overlooked, Wesley and Wesley describe their challenge as follows: "Not a lot of information about the Tigers had been assembled — but through reading books about the early days of the NHL, and scouring newspaper articles, I was able to put together a basic plot of the team's slow rise, and its abrupt decline."[23]

Within these franchise chronicles are the life stories of legendary players and coaches as well as power-wielding managers and owners. And the writers of these team narratives tend to focus on business and marketing exploits of team owners to generate fan interest, gather and keep a talent base, outwit their competitors and adversaries, and ultimately record a winning, or championship record. They tell yarns of organizations struggling to survive in an ever changing and expanding (sometimes over-expanding) market. Of course, this focus on rugged individualism within a hyper-competitive market overlaps with the previously discussed Great Man view of history—and it can also be seen in stories that focus on the quest for the Stanley Cup.

The Quest for the Cup

The Stanley Cup is both an object of desire and symbol of excellence. Its long saga of playoff dramas presents a treasure trove of stories – both actual and mythical – for historians to mine. As journalist William Houston notes: "The Stanley Cup serves as a continuum in the history of the game, a passing of the mantle from one era to another, from one team of hockey players to the next. It is a never-ending legacy, the experience of which is lived vicariously by every child who loves the game, but realized by very few."[24] It is unsurprising that a focus on the various Cup exploits represents another variation of traditional hockey cosmol-

---

22 Sam Wesley with David Wesley, *Hamilton's Hockey Tigers* (Toronto, ON: James Lorimer & Company Ltd., 2005).
23 Ibid., 8.
24 *William Houston,* Pride and Glory: 100 Years of the Stanley Cup (Toronto, ON: McGraw-Hill Ryerson, 1992), xi.

ogy. As hockey historian Henry Hall Roxborough correctly notes: "Right from its origin, there was a strange fascination with the Stanley Cup."[25]

While tales of long ago Cup quests involve famed heroes and link to the business side of the hockey, these are narratives that view history from a different angle. They present the early days of pro hockey as a series of mythical quests, where changes to rules, popularization, and franchise survival were sought through hard-fought battles. Consequently, books in this cluster compile the narratives of 'great men' who have either won or challenged for the Cup in hockey's early days.

A pivotal history of the Cup is Charles L. Coleman's acclaimed three-volume epic, *The Trail of the Stanley Cup* (1964, 1966, 1969).[26] While Coleman's initial volume in the series was published over half a century ago, and was limited to a circulation of 1000, many have cited this work. The series itself recounts details of various Stanley Cup pursuits from its inception in 1892 to 1967. It is a piece of research that places high value on detective work, drawing from historical records, such as contemporary newspaper accounts from Montreal and Toronto. According to historians Morey Holzman and Joseph Nieforth, "No effort in the field of hockey research should go without an acknowledgement of the pioneering efforts of Charles L. Coleman."[27]

Though groundbreaking, Coleman's work did have limitations. As Holzman and Nieforth point out: "Coleman relied heavily upon newspaper accounts for the first volume ... His first major flaw was his failure to recognize the conflicts of interest ... in which the men involved in writing the newspaper reports were involved."[28] Just who were these reporters—and what were their 'individual interests'? Moreover, Coleman "researched only those Canadian newspapers he could obtain at the

---

25 Henry Hall Roxborough, *The Stanley Cup Story* (Toronto, ON: McGraw-Hill Limited Toronto, 1964), 18.
26 See Charles L. Coleman, *The Trail of the Stanley Cup,* Vol. 1, 1893-1926 (Sherbrooke, PQ: Sherbrooke Daily Record Company, NHL, 1964), Charles L. Charles L. Coleman, *The Trail of the Stanley Cup,* Vol. 2, 1927-1946 (Sherbrooke, PQ: Sherbrooke Daily Record Company, NHL, 1966), and Charles L. Coleman, *The Trail of the Stanley Cup,* Vol. 3, 1947-1967 (Sherbrooke, PQ: Sherbrooke Daily Record Company, NHL, 1969).
27 Holzman and Nieforth, *Deceptions and Doublecross*, 16.
28 Ibid.

Montreal and Toronto public libraries."[29] As such, Charles Coleman's 'Cup Quest' narrative is grounded in media reports from Canada's two largest cities, and sets aside the perspectives of journalists from all the other cities and small towns the country.

Another Stanley Cup book appeared in 1964 and was updated and reprinted up to 1971.[30] In *The Stanley Cup Story* (1964), Henry Hall Roxborough provides detailed vignettes of key moments of Cup pursuits across a span of seven decades. As outlined in his acknowledgements, the author drew from library records from across Ontario, McGill University, as well as interviews with various luminaries—including NHL President Clarence S. Campbell, player and entrepreneur Jack Gibson, 'King' Clancy, and 'Cyclone' Taylor.

By no means did histories of the Cup Quest end with Coleman and Roxborough. In 1970, Brian McFarlane (broadcaster and former player) published under the lengthy title: *The Stanley Cup: The Story of the Men and the Teams who for Half a Century Have Fought for Hockey's Most Prized Trophy* (1970).[31] In his acknowledgements, McFarlane tips his hat to both Coleman and Roxborough, but he also sets his own work apart, telling readers that he "has delved deeply into newspaper accounts of games compiled by three Toronto papers, the *Star, the Globe and Mail, and the Telegram.*"[32] Later, he punctuates the importance of the Stanley Cup as a historic marker, sharing a whirlwind of fantastical legends, such as the time the Cup was drop kicked into the Rideau Canal, the occasion it was forgotten at a player's house, and the day it was left behind on a sidewalk as a group of players drove away.[33]

Additional books on the 'Cup Quest' have appeared over the years, including Dan Diamond's *Official National Hockey League Stanley Cup*

---

29 Ibid.

30 Roxborough, *The Stanley Cup Story*, 1964. Updated editions were published in 1966, 1968, and 1971.

31 Brian McFarlane, *The Stanley Cup: The Story of the Men and the Teams who for Half a Century Have Fought for Hockey's Most Prized Trophy* (Toronto, ON: Pagurian Press Limited, 1970). McFarlane has updated this book on numerous occasions with different titles, including: *Stanley Cup Fever* (1978), *Stanley Cup Fever: 100 Years of Hockey Greatness* (1992), *Stanley Cup Fever: More than a Century of Hockey Greatness* (1999), *Legendary Stanley Cup Stories* (2009).

32 McFarlane, *The Stanley Cup*, 1970, vii.

33 These events reputedly occurred in 1905, 1906, and 1924. See Ibid., ix-xi.

Centennial Book (1992), D'Arcy Jenish's *Stanley Cup: One Hundred Years of Hockey at its Best* (1992), William Houston's *Pride and Glory: 100 Years of the Stanley Cup* (1992), and Eric Zwieg's *Stanley Cup: 120 Years of Hockey Supremacy* (2014). Like Homer's great *Odyssey*, tales – such as the Dawson City Nuggets' 4000-mile journey to challenge Ottawa for the Cup in 1905 – are told time and time again in various renditions—forming a quest-oriented version of the Great Man history narrative.[34] Yet viewing history through such a lens urges readers to perceive pro hockey's genesis as a parade of champions and contenders. Although this makes for entertaining reading, it leaves out the narratives of all of those players, teams, owners, and cities that never seriously contended for the Cup. While the lore of the Cup is an engaging history it is an incomplete one nevertheless.

The Great Saga

Some hockey historians depict a wider landscape of the genesis of pro hockey and the NHL, yet they still largely subscribe to the Great Man history narrative. These books have chronicled a combination of aspects of the League's birth, development, and expansion over the years. Books in this cluster also tackle such topics as the waxing and waning of fan interest, attendance records, revenues, rule changes, and team standings.

In 1967, the NHL's fiftieth anniversary, a new hockey chronicle appeared in bookshops. Entitled *50 Years of Hockey: An Intimate History of the National Hockey League*, the book was an epic account of the league's history.[35] Written by Brian McFarlane, the book includes a very brief segment on the time that preceded the formation of the NHL as well as the league's early years. McFarlane regards the era as a time of mystery—and while he offers readers an origin story of the NHL, it is a very

---

34 Fictional accounts of early hockey history include: Don Reddick, Dawson City Seven (Fredericton, NB: Goose Lane Editions, 1993) as well as Eric Zweig, *Hockey Night in the Dominion of Canada* (Toronto, ON: Lester Publishing Limited, 1992).

35 Brian McFarlane, *50 Years of Hockey: An Intimate History of the National Hockey League* (Toronto, ON: Pagurian Press Limited, 1967), x. McFarlane would later update the book as *60 Years of Hockey: The Intimate Story Behind North America's Fastest, Most Exciting Sport. Complete Statistics and Records* (Toronto, ON: McGraw-Hill Ryerson Company, 1976) and *100 Years of Hockey* (Toronto, ON: Deneau, 1989).

brief one.

Similar to McFarlane, author, documentary filmmaker, and screen-writer Michael McKinley has released numerous epics that discuss the overall history of hockey. These books include: *Putting a Roof on Winter: Hockey's Rise from Sport to Spectacle* (2000), the coffee table tome, *Hockey: A People's History* (2006), and the more recent publication, *It's Our Game: Celebrating 100 Years of Hockey Canada* (2014).[36] Because many of his books survey the long history of the sport, McKinley often focuses his gaze on the early years of pro hockey. He presents the sport on a larger scale—and in doing so he focuses on key personalities, events, and ups-and-downs of different franchises and dramas behind Stanley Cup quests.

Yet McKinley presses further and addresses various issues of exclusion and discrimination in hockey history, as visible in *Hockey: A People's History*. When describing Montreal's first francophone club (the Nationals) and its Irish-Catholic club (the Montagnards), he observes that neither team challenged for the Stanley Cup in the late 1890s and early 1900s because "They were never admitted to the English leagues [...] so the prize remained out of reach."[37] He dedicates a few paragraphs to sketch out women's organized hockey in the 1890s and later devotes a few paragraphs to African-Canadian hockey in the early 1900s—noting that it was a "racist attitude that segregated maritime hockey."[38]

After briefly outlining a growing interest in women's hockey during the First World War, McKinley observes that: "When the war ended, so did the craze for women's hockey. It would be another two decades, in the prelude to another world war, before women's hockey once again captured national attention."[39] Retelling the Hamilton Tigers strike of 1925, McKinley bluntly states: "The last thing [NHL President] Calder and the NHL owners needed as they advanced into the brave new American market was an ugly public labour dispute, and so the NHL did some-

---

36 Michael McKinley, Hockey: A People's History (Toronto, ON: McClelland & Stewart, 2006). Also see Michael McKinley, *Putting A Roof on Winter: Hockey's Rise from Sport to Spectacle* (Toronto, ON: Greystone Books, 2002) and Michael McKinley, *It's Our Game: Celebrating 100 Years of Hockey Canada* (Toronto, ON: Viking, 2014).

37 McKinley, *Hockey: A People's History*, 2006, 24-25.

38 Ibid., 26.

39 Ibid., 80.

thing ugly to crush their upstart players."[40]

When discussing hockey during the Great Depression, McKinley tells the story of Alec Antoine and the Alkali Lake Braves, a team comprised of members of the Shuswap Nation. Describing the team's travels, he notes that when playing in the town of Williams Lake, the players on the team "were barred from staying in a hotel, or eating in a restaurant, by the colour barrier."[41] As a consequence the team needed to pitch tents near the outdoor rink and sleep outside. It was a time, McKinley states, "when aboriginal children were being forcibly removed from their homes and placed into white-run residential schools."[42] In 1931, the team won a Northern B.C. amateur title and traveled to Vancouver to "play two matches against a team of all-stars selected from the semi-professional Commercial League."[43] While the games were close, the Braves lost both matches. And the response of the Vancouver press, McKinley observes, was "typical of the attitudes of the time, [and] assessed the Braves' performance by making it racial."[44] Illustrating his point, McKinley quotes from the *Vancouver Sun*, which curtly states that: "They are still a primitive people, these silent, shadowy folk of the northland and they take their sport in the same way."[45]

Although these vignettes do not take up a large part of McKinley's extensive text, they shed light on aspects of hockey history that have all too often gone unmentioned—its legacy of exclusion. In this sense, the writer is helping to draw attention to the silenced stories of the past. McKinley pays attention to way larger injustices in Canada took form in the country's hockey landscape. He is the first major hockey historian to draw attention to multiple issues of racism and sexism in hockey's early days. While McKinley does not shy away from discussing social issues in the sport, they are not central to his narrative. Consequently, we might say that his writing straddles both traditional and alternative approaches to hockey history. And to find a more detailed picture of inequality

---

40 Ibid., 90-91
41 Ibid., 106-107.
42 Ibid., 107.
43 Ibid.
44 Ibid., 108.
45 Ibid.

in hockey's early days, we need to turn to historians who focus on the sociological dimensions of the sport's history.

Expanding the Cosmology

Over the past two decades, newer works on the origins of pro hockey have challenged the existing conservative hockey cosmology in a way that it's expanded. These books, for the most part, are sagas that depict hockey as a space where exclusion lurks within the culture of the sport itself. And these publications examine persistent social issues entangled with both hockey and Canadian society at large, including racism, sexism, and classism. Sometimes, these more recent historians have explored hockey leagues as organizations within an inequitable society—and other times, they have discussed how hockey leagues themselves reproduce (or even extend) social inequities.

A number of hockey historians view the sport as a labour landscape—one that, at times, is a space of conflict between the rights of workers and interests of management. In *Hamilton's Hockey Tigers*, David and Sam Wesley describe a key event as a labour battle. After all, the 1925 Hamilton Tigers are the only NHL team to go on strike. And the writers take a critical view of the NHL's early days, a time when unionized employees were overpowered by franchise owners and league executives. Placing the conflict in a social context, the writers note that: "the Hamilton Tigers is a paradigm of the turbulence, the spectacle, recklessness, volatility, and charm of the 1920's Hamilton as a whole."[46] In summing up the affair they state: "in retrospect, perhaps it was the character of the city of Hamilton itself—that of strong labour, of mobsters, of the willingness to stand firm, despite a deficiency in size, against powers with greater population, dollars, or influence—that led to the Tigers' demise."[47] The two writers focus on a slice of the NHL's primordial period; and they illustrate how pro hockey was a space where the rights of players (who were also workers) were often at cross-purposes with the goals of man-

---

[46] Wesley with Wesley, *Hamilton's Hockey Tigers*, 2005, 8.
[47] Ibid., 8.

agement.

In the early 2000s Morey Holzman and Joseph Nieforth published a thoughtful work on labour, power and hockey history. Entitled *Deceptions and Doublecross: How the NHL Conquered Hockey* (2002), the writers focus on the larger narrative of multiple franchises, owners, and the pro leagues themselves within the volatile, topsy-turvy worlds of the NHA (later the NHL) and PCHA (later the WCHL and WHL).[48] Holzman and Nieforth methodically examine the interlocking team sagas that unfolded during the 1910s and 1920s—paying close attention to the fractious relationships of owners and executives (such as Eddie Livingstone and Frank Calder). In discussing the dealings and conflicts of these various power-holders, the writers draw a sharp picture of the competitive, dishonest, and litigious world that shaped pro hockey's early years. It was not at all a romantic time of innocence. In this sense, the book adds something very unique to traditional hockey cosmology.

Deceptions and Doublecross is not simply an origin story driven by 'great' heroes, moguls, and/or men on mythical 'Cup Quests.' It is a history that shows the inner workings of evolving pro hockey leagues—social systems of allegiances, alliances and betrayals. In developing this new narrative, the two writers combed press reports from Canada and the U.S., as well as league and court documents. Their work reshapes the Great Man cosmology by shedding light on the mysterious circumstances surrounding the development and growth pro hockey and the NHL. While the writers draw from newspaper accounts, they also put forward a healthy skepticism of the media—and in doing so, they disentangle alignments between franchise owners, media tycoons, and sportswriters, such as Elmer Ferguson, Tommy Gorman, and John Ross Robertson. The book delves into the era that led up to and immediately followed the NHL's creation, illuminating a period that had previously been clouded with legend and mystery. Ultimately, the genesis of pro hockey is presented not simply as an era of 'great men' but rather a time where powerbrokers constructed a system firmly grounded in capitalism and competi-

---

48 The NHA transformed into the NHL in 1917. The PCHA formed in 1911 and in 1924 it merged with (and became) the Western Coast Hockey League (WCHL). The WCHL was renamed the Western Hockey League (WHL) in 1925 and disbanded in 1926. See Holzman and Nieforth, *Deceptions and Doublecross*, 2002.

tion—a system where players were seen and treated as chattel.

Academic John Wong contributes to the ever-shifting cosmology of pro hockey with *Lords of the Rinks: The Emergence of the National Hockey League 1875-1936* (2005). The scholarly work adds detail to the monetary- and power-oriented view of the sport's history. Throughout the work, Wong culls from a variety of sources, including Stanley Cup Regulations (published in 1903), the National Hockey Association Constitution (formulated in 1910), the NHL's Binding Agreement of 1926, as well as various gate receipt records. He focuses on regional interests and hockey markets as well as expansion into the U.S. and the development of a minor league system. "By examining commercial and professional hockey through a network of stakeholders," Wong states, "I hope to provide a broader perspective of the hockey industry."[49] Yet there are limitations to his work—and as Wong himself admits, his approach led him to set aside certain voices, or stories. As such, Wong's chronicle, leaves out the stories of "hockey played by women and by non-whites, and that in lower-level organizations."[50] Consequently, while Wong delves into the power systems of pro hockey and the NHL in its early years, he recognizes that this limits his chronicle to white men, which marked only a portion of Canadian society in the early 1900s.

Challenging and Expanding the Cosmology

Over the years, traditional hockey cosmologies have left out various perspectives. For instance, the narratives of Canada's Anishinaabe, women, and African-Canadians have commonly been left out of pro hockey's origin stories. Yet, in recent years a few writers have drawn attention to these gaps—and have begun the process of recovering these stories.

While documentary filmmaker Don Marks wrote *They Call Me Chief: Warriors on Ice: The Story of Indians in the NHL* (2008) academic Michael A. Robindoux penned *Stickhandling through the Margins: First Nations Hockey in Canada* (2012). Marks, gathered the oral stories of a number of An-

49 John Wong, *Lords of the Rinks: The Emergence of the National Hockey League* 1875-1936 (Toronto, ON: University of Toronto Press, 2005), 4.
50 Ibid., 5.

ishinaabe players and one coach while making a film. As Marks notes: "The contributions and involvement of Canada's First Nation people in a sport such as hockey, a game they may have invented, has been mostly overlooked."[51] Human Kinetics Professor Robidoux developed his book after living and playing hockey with "people of the Esketemc First Nation and the Sandy Lake First Nation."[52] In Robidoux' view, "First Nations hockey is a celebration of diversity and heterogeneity in the face of global homogeneity."[53] Given that Canada's original people could not even vote in federal elections until 1960, and are still, in a formal legal sense, 'wards of the state'—the persistent disregard of Anishinaabe hockey history is unfortunately unsurprising.

With the growth of women's hockey and its acceptance as a Winter Olympic sport for the 1998 Nagano Olympics some hockey historians were compelled to look at women's hockey experiences. In *Proud Past, Bright Future: One Hundred Years of Canadian Women's Hockey* (1994), Brian McFarlane begins in the 1800s, and bounds through the successes and barriers faced by women's hockey. Regarding the time of the NHL's inception, he states: "As late as 1914, the Amateur Athletic Union of Canada wouldn't allow women to take part in the sports or activities they controlled."[54] Later, educator Wayne Norton published *Women on Ice: The Early Years of Women's Hockey in Western Canada* (2009).[55] Focusing on the story of the Vancouver Amazons, Norton discusses the team's interactions with the Patrick brothers, who discussed forming a women's hockey league to compliment the PCHA in the mid-1910s. Norton sees his work as addressing a gap in the literature on hockey history. At one point, he notes that: "This particular history of women's ice hockey in western Canada was undertaken many years later than ideally it should

51 Don Marks, *They Call Me Chief: Warriors on Ice* (Winnipeg, MB: J. Gordon Shillingford Publishing, 2008), 25.
52 Michael A. Robidoux, *Stickhandling through the Margins* (Toronto, ON: University of Toronto Press, 2012), ix.
53 Ibid., 151.
54 Brian McFarlane, *Proud Past, Bright Future: One Hundred Years of Canadian Women's Hockey* (Toronto, ON: Stoddart, 1995), 45.
55 Wayne Norton, *Women on Ice: The Early Years of Women's Hockey in Western Canada* (Vancouver, BC: Ronsdale Press, 2009).

have been."[56]

In *Black Ice: The Lost History of the Coloured Hockey Hockey League of the Maritimes,* 1895-1925 (2004), George and Darril Fosty chronicle a too-often neglected aspect of the sport's history in Canada—the African-Canadian hockey experience. Recognizing this gap in hockey history literature, the writers state: "Our knowledge of the roots of Canadian hockey have been based almost solely on the historical records maintained by early white historians."[57] According to George and Darril Fosty, "The roots of modern Canadian hockey originate, in large part, from the influence of an even more surprising source, that of early African-Canadian hockey."[58] Stressing this gap in hockey's documented history, the writers state that while "Today there are no monuments to the Colored Hockey League of the Maritimes and few hockey books even recognize the league."[59] Because so little remains in the way of indicators or reminders of this league – and this narrative – pro hockey's origin stories need to push beyond the confines of the NHL and its parent and sibling leagues.

With these silenced stories in mind, it is vital that hockey chroniclers take a critical eye to the sport and ask the uncomfortable question: *What is Canada's history of exclusion, and how does it form a part of professional and amateur hockey in past and present contexts?*

Shifting Hockey Cosmology

Some newer historians put forward a view that illustrates hockey's legacy of exclusion and inequity. And while these writers indicate how the sport, in some ways, binds Canada together, they also illustrate how the sport divides the country. These writers have helped sharpen our understanding of the birth of pro hockey in relation to acts of deception, stakeholder perspectives, decision-making processes, and, perhaps most

---

56 Norton, 2009, 7.

57 George Fosty and Darril Fosty, *Black Ice: The Lost History of the Colored Hockey League of the Maritimes,* 1895-1925 (New York, NY: Stryker-Indigo Publishing Company, 2004), 2.

58 Ibid., 2.

59 Ibid., 196. To read more about African-Canadian hockey narratives, also see Cecil Harris, *Breaking the Ice: The Black Experience in Professional Hockey* (London, ON: Insomniac Press, 2004).

importantly, the way early twentieth-century hockey culture was tightly interlocked with social issues that were deeply rooted in Canada at the time. While earlier, more traditional, hockey historians strived to gather stories and map out a past, some more recent writers have sought to rewrite the narrative—forming alternatives to the traditional hockey cosmology.

One More History

A fresh stack of hockey histories has appeared on bookshelves as the NHL approaches its centennial. Perhaps the most well-known of these publications is the one penned by former Prime Minister, Stephen J. Harper. Unsurprisingly, the release of a sports chronicle by a (then) current Head of State garnered enormous publicity in Canada and raised a few eyebrows abroad. Given that this book has received so much attention, I will focus on it in the final segment of this chapter. Throughout *A Great Game: The Forgotten Leafs and the Rise of Professional Hockey* (2013), Harper puts forward an early history of Ontario's transition from amateur to professional hockey—with a focus on Toronto.[60] While it is certainly a new book, the question remains: *Is this an alternative to, or a new variation of the traditional Great Man hockey cosmology?*

A Great Game:

In *A Great Game: The Forgotten Leafs and the Rise of Professional Hockey*, Stephen Harper chronicles the shift from amateur to professional hockey in Ontario in the early 1900s. The transition was not a smooth one. It was a spectacle filled with conflict, confrontations, and fierce adversaries—including John Ross Robertson, 'Doc' Gibson, and William Hewitt. Teams came and went. Leagues rose up and crumbled. Toronto struggled to contend for the Cup—and after years the city made its first challenge

---

60 See Stephen J. Harper, *A Great Game: The Forgotten Leafs and the Rise of Professional Hockey* (Toronto, ON: Simon & Schuster, 2013). Also see Craig H. *Bowlsby, 1913: The Year They Invented the Future of Hockey* (Vancouver, BC: Knights of Winter, 2013) and D'Arcy Jenish, *The NHL: 100 Years of On-Ice Action and Boardroom Battles* (Toronto, ON: Doubleday Canada, 2013).

and eventually won. The period is ripe for storytelling—and it is this story that sits at the heart of Harper's account.

Following the paths of such scribes as Cosentino as well as Holzman and Nieforth, Harper adds detail to the decades that preceded the formation of the NHL and saw the sport split into amateur and pro hockey factions. The book disentangles a complicated narrative where packs of powerful foes fought for control over the direction of hockey in Ontario—and contended over who had claim to moral leverage. Yet while Harper fills in key gaps and presents numerous events in their social context he also perpetuates myths and neglects to capture critical aspects of the social context he portrays.

Harper dispels a number of age-old myths and recovers lost details from history linked to pro hockey's early days. When discussing Toronto's early Cup challengers, for instance, he asks: "Who were these Stanley Cup contenders and what happened to them? ... So determined—and successful—would be their naysayers in obliterating their existence that even their name would be long forgotten."[61] Regarding the Toronto Blue Shirts, he makes a call for historical revisionism: "It remains to this day the only one of the city's pro hockey championships not to have its banner hung in the Air Canada Centre."[62] He aims to recover their story. Describing the tragic star forward Bruce Ridpath, Harper pines: "Bound for the Hockey Hall of Fame" before a terrible car accident, he was "the ultimate "forgotten Leaf."[63] In some regards, Harper recovers the neglected narratives of John Ross Robertson and Bruce Ridpath, as well as other nearly forgotten hockey figures from the early 1900s.

On numerous occasions, Harper presents hockey events within the frame of their larger social context. This context was rooted in the Victorian and Edwardian views of those who held power in the leagues across Ontario. He describes the landscape as an "order" that "would reflect the exclusively British, bourgeois character of these Ontario organizers, and from the outset it had a distinctly puritanical and authoritarian

---

61 Ibid., xiii.
62 Ibid., 272.
63 Ibid., 281.

streak."[64] Discussing the matter of sponsorship, Harper notes that: "the prohibition on pay was just a thin veneer covering deeper issues of class and racism. Athletes who most required pay were those who tended to come from underprivileged or ethnic backgrounds."[65] In short, amateur sports status was something only the privileged could afford. Yet while the book clearly aims to fill-in historical gaps and make connections to its larger social landscape, it perpetuates myths and neglects to delve deeply into its social milieu.

Harper perpetuates the myth that the NHL's Original Six era as one of unique stability. The early years of the NHL, Harper states, were "marked by rapid salary escalation, pools of red ink for management and franchise instability. On the other hand, there have been times of remarkable consistency—most notably the quarter century of the NHL Original Six."[66] The view Harper puts forward here is rooted in popular belief. But is it accurate? Was the Original Six Era truly a time of "remarkable consistency"? NHL documents seem to indicate otherwise. In fact, the 1942-1967 era was a time when some team owners were struggling and the survival of certain franchises was very much in doubt, as Board of Governor meeting minutes indicate.[67]

Additionally, although Harper's writing offers a portrait of the social milieu of Ontario in the early 1900s it is, at times, a cursory picture— one that misses out on key details. At various points, Harper discusses context, pointing out hockey's interlocking relationship with the wider sociological sphere. Yet his description of that interlocking relationship presents a limited picture. In the first chapter of his book, for instance, Harper depicts Toronto in the early 1900s. But what kind of picture does he paint? He states that: "These were good times to be raising a family in the Ontario capital."[68] Here, it seems that Harper's view of the past is tinted with feelings of nostalgia. Yet for whom were these "good times"? Women? Men? African-Canadians? Working-class Torontonians? This

---

64 Ibid., 13.
65 Ibid., 21.
66 Harper, *A Great Game*, 286.
67 See Jenish, *The NHL*, 2013
68 Harper, *A Great Game*, 2.

was an era of racism and institutionalized racial segregation, residential schooling, rampant anti-Semitism, and systemic sexism. Neither women nor Canada's original people were legally seen as persons and neither could vote in elections. While early 1900s Toronto may have been comfortable for a certain segment of the city's population, they were by no means "good times" for everyone.

When placing the hockey world of Toronto within its larger sociological context, Harper claims: "A British Canada, Toronto believed, needed the unequivocal British leadership that only it could provide."[69] Yet if Toronto was not purely British (or even supportive of 'British ideals'), can we infer that the entire city believed in "British leadership"? Readers are left to wonder what exactly Harper means by this. Later, when Harper mentions how John Ross Robertson engaged in racist and sexist views and language he neglects to discuss the pervasive nature of racism and sexism of the time.[70] In fact, he makes the claim that Robertson was both racist and anti-racist, stating: "He was also an ardent British imperialist ... an antiracist, antislavery advocate who regularly employed racial slurs."[71] Yet how does Harper define antiracism? To support the assertion that Robertson was an antiracist who also "regularly employed racial slurs" Harper would need to explain his reasoning, which he neglects to do. Without addressing the social issues of injustice of the era, Harper's account is aligned with the traditional view of hockey cosmology.

When describing Toronto, Harper briefly refers to the hardships endured by those who lived in the city's "foreign district" in the early 1900s.[72] Yet he does not delve into what those hardships entailed. And while he describes the debate over Tom Longboat's amateur status, he does not discuss the racism that Canada's Anishinaabe people endured at the time—which aligns the book with more traditional conservative narratives of hockey history.[73] Some may counter that *A Great Game* is

---

69 Ibid., 7.
70 Ibid., 124.
71 Ibid., 24
72 Ibid., 3.
73 Ibid., 119, 163, 175.

a book about hockey and does not need to delve into such matters—yet Harper himself makes mention of social issues throughout his writing, but in a way that leaves them on the periphery. So, while Harper acknowledges that Toronto (and indeed Canada) was an unjust and inequitable society in the early twentieth century, he neglects to dig deeply into those issues, perhaps done with some intent. By ignoring structural issues around race and racism, class and classism, he is able to shift at the conceptual level the problems of individuals (e.g., poverty) on to individuals themselves, all of which is consistent with a conservative ideological perspective. Great men, use hardships to develop character; great countries become great through rugged individuals battling through hardship and struggle, or, so the argument goes.

So, when Harper writes how individuals coped with issues of poverty in Toronto at the turn of the 20th century, he makes special mention that they relied on "extended families, neighborhood interests and, especially religious institutions."[74] He seems to be saying that back in the Golden Age, people were a lot more independent, self-reliant, demonstrated much more resiliency, and had a kind of tenacity not reflected in today's population; and most importantly they of course did not have to rely on government handouts. Unfortunately, from this perspective, implicit in Harper's statement is that people today are soft, dependent, and to easily persuaded to rely on government handouts to cope with life's hardships. He goes on to write, with some notable sense of disdain, that "nothing like the government payments and social services of our age existed," back then.[75]

Not surprisingly then, Harper devotes much attention to the biographies of key figures in Ontario's amateur and pro hockey landscape. Consequently, his writing is very much a big-man view of the past. While Harper recognizes the influence of financial interests on the development of sport as a spectacle, he does so by outlining the stories of a select few 'Great Men.' While he fills-in some gaps, and explores key aspects of the Victorian and Edwardian attitudes that prompted some hockey

[74] Ibid., 3.
[75] Ibid.

barons to oppose the rise of hockey professionalism, a number of these points have been made before.[76] Although he makes important connections between the growth and transformation of hockey amidst a largely traditional world, he neglects to delve into the socio-political landscape of the day. Harper recognizes that early 1900s Canada was a time of "deeper issues of class and racism" and was shaped by power-holders who held an "authoritarian streak."[77] He attempts to point out a few of the inequities at hand. Yet his writing plays fast and loose with history as it does not in any meaningful way present a deep or thoughtful exploration of the social milieu at play. While *A Great Game* casts light on an often-neglected era in hockey history, it functions to once again promote a much older and much more conservative hockey cosmology.

Conclusion

Every year, a new batch of hockey histories appears on bookshelves, offering varying portrayals of the sport's mysterious beginnings. Some of these writers tend to follow the traditional hockey cosmology rooted in the Great Man theory of history. They present the past as a landscape populated by rugged men toughing it out, battling wits, words, and fists with one another for fame and fortune. As time has passed, a growing number of historians have expanded their lens, to include such aspects as franchise dramas, the quest for the elusive Stanley Cup, and the great hockey saga. And these aspects of the sport have remained firmly rooted in, and constricted by, a Great Man-oriented view of the past. Yet some have pushed beyond this view.

Over the past few decades a growing number of hockey historians have challenged the conservative, Great Man view of the sport's origins, and indeed Canada itself. A survey of hockey chronicles reveals that more and more historians have cast their eyes back to the primordial age of professional hockey and posed uncomfortable questions about such social matters as racism, sexism, and classism. In putting forward fresh

---

76 See, for instance, Cosentino, *Renfrew Millionaires,* 1990.
77 Harper, *A Great Game,* 21, 13.

alternatives to the traditional hockey cosmology, these newer thinkers have shed light on issues of exclusion, inequity, and social justice. These different views and versions of hockey cosmology not only tell us about the origins of pro hockey but they also say something about the shifting way we (as Canadians) have perceived – and indeed portrayed – our own history over the years. Ultimately, by better understanding the way we portray our past – in all its complexities – we can better grasp the nature of our history as well as our present.

CHAPTER TWO:
Hockey Men in Canada: Men, Masculinities and Hockey Culture

"My game is a contact sport. It's a game of men."[78]

Marcel Provost
Professional hockey player (1950-1970)

Introduction

Hockey is a game of men, as the above quote from Marcel Provost suggests, but it is also a game of masculinities. In this chapter, while I do focus on men, I pay much more attention to the production of Canadian hockey masculinities within hockey communities and culture. Using the analytical tools and insights provided by sociologist Raewyn Connell's work on men and masculinities,[79] and drawing from various hockey related autobiographies, biographies, and sources found in the popular media, I explore how prevailing gender norms function within hockey communities and culture to promote and produce a dominant and prevailing model of Canadian masculinity, the adoption of which, may not be in the best interests of men and boys, women and girls.

Much ink has been spilled and much has been said about the benefits

---

78 Marcel Provost, *Marcel Provost: A Life in Hockey* (Windsor, ON: Biblioasis, 2015), 69.
79 R. W. Connell, *Masculinities* (Los Angeles, CA: University of California Press, 1995).

that come to children, in particular boys, when they play organized hockey. Hockey promoters, for instance, often suggest that it is a place and space to provide exercise, build character, teach self-discipline, learn how to play as an individual within a team, and develop virtues such as perseverance and fortitude. All of which, to some degree or another, is true, and most Canadian hockey communities concerned about developing their young boys would find it hard to reject an organization that espouses and publicizes these particular virtues. But there is much more boys learn in the culture of organized hockey than this.[80] And by this I mean the deeper attitudes, practices, and values that are implanted and nourished within hockey communities and culture. Grounded in the knowledge that hockey is among the key socializing forces in the development of young boys in Canada, they also learn important, and deeper lessons that have the potential to bring themselves and others physical, emotional and psychological harm.[81] Drawing on a broad evidentiary base, and as this chapter will demonstrate, what boys also learn from being immersed in hockey communities and culture from a young age is far more complicated, and potentially worrisome, than initially assumed. It is too these important issues and complexities that I now turn.

In Canada, no sport is so closely associated with an appropriate model of masculinity than ice hockey. Certainly, other major sports such as baseball and basketball and football are linked to the production of values closely associated with dominant models of masculinity such as aggression and competitiveness but no sport reaches the same elevated status in Canada as men's professional hockey. This claim makes more sense when we understand that team sports that are gendered hyper-masculine such as ice hockey and infused with violence sit atop the gendered hierarchy, while non-violent and non-contact sports such as badminton, ballet, gymnastics and golf sit on the bottom, often

---

80 The word culture comes from the Latin word, *cultura*, which means 'to grow.'
81 Kristi A. Allain, "'Real Fast and Tough': The Construction of Canadian Hockey Masculinity," *Sociology of Sport Journal*, 25 (2008), 468.

considered by men as sports for "sissies."[82] In fact, violence in hockey should not be seen as an anomaly or something that occasionally happens, circling its periphery, but in many ways is best understood as its very essence.[83] Fighting, boarding, crosschecking, spearing, charging, blocking, and dropping the gloves and fighting is not discouraged, but encouraged, although when caught, penalized.

In a 1945 essay, "The Sporting Spirit", George Orwell argued, "Serious sport has nothing to do with fair play. It is bound up with hatred, jealousy, boastfulness, disregard for all rules and sadistic pleasure in witnessing violence; in other words it is war minus the shooting."[84] Although Orwell was talking about boxing and English football, he just might as well have been talking about hockey. The normalization of violence across hockey communities and culture is, to some measure war-like, and reflected in the way in which it is constructed as just 'part of the game.' One very early but excellent research study on youth ice hockey players demonstrated how violence became normative behaviour within men's hockey communities and culture. As the study indicated, hockey players who establish a reputation for being an aggressive "hitter" more or less secures them a level of status in the hockey communities, and certainly among his peers.[85] Reflecting how violence has become over time just 'part of the game,' former NHL player Dave 'Tiger' Williams declared, "you consent to assault when you lace up

---

82 *National Post* writer Christie Blatchford, in an article titled, "Where Have All the Manly Men Gone? Toronto, City of Sissies," argued that today's men are no longer as manly as men from Canada's past. Her argument rested on her observation of young boys greeting each other affectionately and warmly with hugs, instead of with aggression and presumably with fists and punches. Blatchford went on to say that the today's 'feminized' men (and boys) lack masculinity because they no longer play aggressive contact sports, preferring non-contact, 'femininzed' sports such as badminton instead, a sport for 'sissies'. See, Christie Blatchford, "Where Have All the Manly Men Gone? Toronto, City of Sissies", *National Post*, December 10, 2011, A29.
83 See, for example, Michael Atkinson, "It's Still Part of the Game: Violence and Masculinity in Canadian Ice Hockey, in *Sexual Sports Rhetoric: Historical and Media Context of Violence*, edited by Linda K Fuller (New York, NY: Peter Lang, 2010).
84 George Orwell, "The Sporting Spirit," in *George Orwell: Essays* (New York, NY: Alfred A. Knopf, 2002), 969.
85 See, M. D. Smith, "Significant Other Influences on the Assaultive Behaviour of Young Hockey Players," *International Review of Sport Sociology* 3-4 (9) 1974, 45-58. See, also, W. R. McMurtry, *Investigation and Inquiry into Violence in Amateur Hockey* (Ottawa: Ministry of Community and Social Services, 1974).

your skates. It's what hockey is all about."[86] The brutal truth revealed by Williams is that the violence that occurs on the ice rink would be judged as criminal in another playing area or in the street. Hockey cultures become problematic when young men begin to internalize the lessons promoted within these cultures; the pressure to embody and conform to the dominant characteristics of a potentially violent hyper-masculinity.

Violent, high status sports often serve as a key zones for the expression of patriarchal practices and a place for boys to be viewed by other boys as 'appropriately' masculine. Similar to the association between football and a so called 'appropriate' American masculinity, the historical prominence of hockey within Canada's popular media and political and folk culture, reminds us that professional hockey remains the arena 'par excellence', the place and space, in which young Canadian boys/men can prove their masculinity. This sort of historical prominence and elevated status has successfully sustained an exalted model of masculinity that prioritizes hyper-competitiveness, hyper-aggressiveness, violence, and superiority over women and deep respect for and compliance with men's authority.[87] To put a little more succinctly, the hierarchal and highly competitive and hyper-aggressive world of men's professional hockey, largely empty of women and fuelled by masculine fantasies, is an important key site for the construction and reproduction of an idealized version of Canadian masculinity that is closely associated with values that, to some measure, work against the best interest of men and boys, women and girls.

Set against the widespread cultural influence of hockey in Canada

---

86 Jeff Miller and Mike Helka, "Has Fighting Become Outdated?" *The Spokesman Review*, May 11, 2004, C1, C4.

87 Recent autobiographies have drawn our attention to the potential horrific outcomes for some boys who are placed under the supervision of some male authorities within the hockey context. See, for example, Sheldon Kennedy with James Grainger, *Why I Didn't Say Anything* (London, ON: Insomniac Press, 2011); see also, Theo Fleury, with Kirstie McLellan Day, *Playing with Fire: The Highest Highs and The Lowest Lows of Theo Fleury* (Toronto, ON: HarperCollins Publishers, 2011). Former professional player Patrick O'Sullivan recently documented his horrific experiences with his father growing up as a talented young hockey player. See also, Patrick O'Sullivan with Gare Joyce, *Breaking Away: A Harrowing Story of Resilience, Courage and Triumph* (Toronto, ON: HarperCollins, 2015).

that sometimes verges on a mania, a so-called 'idealized' Canadian hockey masculinity is defined by various characteristics, but none so prominent or as powerful as being fearless and aggressive. These attributes are privileged in many ways over what is "considered to be more effeminate ways" of expressing an acceptable hockey masculinity such as through a proficiency at "skating, passing, and other skilled maneuvers."[88] No doubt that to be highly proficient in skating, passing and shooting for example is important and integral to being a high-quality hockey player, but within Canadian hockey community and culture, a player, most of all, has to be fearless and hyper-aggressive. It is a sport that so many of us, as parents and as men and women and children, support financially and emotionally, the players we tend to most idolize and cheer on, are those who are able to demonstrate a style of play that is defined by their fearlessness and capacity for hyper-aggressive play. This is precisely why in many hockey games fans routinely encourage and cheer on violent fistfights between players. Male players who 'have guts,' 'who never back down from a fight,' and who otherwise are consistently hyper-aggressive are illustrative and exemplary examples of the success of the prevailing gender system and its values and definitions of masculinity found in hockey communities and cultures. An unfortunate outcome of these displays of hyper-masculine behaviour is that from a very young age, no doubt, many young boys who witness such gendered interactions take away the idea that in order to be masculine one has to be dominant over other men and fighting becomes a legitimate form of conflict resolution.

At the same time, being able to dominate other men, physically or otherwise, is a key marker of a so-called 'appropriate' masculinity. A male hockey player's gendered identity is constructed through fighting and aggressive play, both of which are connected closely to external gendered rewards: honour, prestige, and status. Within hockey culture it is not possible for a player to skate away from a fight without seri-

---

[88] Allain, "Real Fast," 13.

ously compromising his masculinity. After backing away from a fight during a game, former NHLer Derek Sanderson's father scolded him for being weak, telling him, "Never back away from a fight … Never!"[89] Honour lost on the ice, means an emasculated hockey player, and an emasculated hockey player is no hockey player at all, so the logic goes. All of which has fortified the association between masculinity, hockey and violence. It now goes without saying, in the context of ice hockey, by demonstrating a hyper-aggressive masculinity, one that is based on one's differing levels and capacities for violence in a way that makes him dominant over all others, a player is afforded forms of masculine honour. The late Derek Boogard, the Minnesota Wild's former designated fighter who played pro-hockey from 2005-2011, never really scored more than a few points in an entire season. Yet his replica jersey used to outsell the vast majority of his high-scoring teammates. Although he did not like to fight on the rink, for his willingness to fight, Boogaard was beloved by almost everyone, especially fans. They certainly thought he was a warrior. In fact, merely engaging in various forms of violence that reflect a battle ready "warrior" attitude can bestow masculine honour and privilege. Derek Sanderson, for instance, recalled a gendered lesson he learned from his father: "My dad made getting stitches seem like the red badge of courage, so whenever I got cut, I just kept playing. And I noticed that when you do that in hockey, people can't believe it. You get attention."[90] Sanderson's reflection is helpful in reminding us that hockey, in the past and today, remains a key site - a place and space - that functions as a key site for the mobilization of an appropriate Canadian hockey masculinity, one that takes seriously a man's capacity to engage in various forms of violence.

As I have been arguing, in the Canadian context, men and boys are routinely seduced by forms of patriarchal rewards such as masculine honour and prestige and status that operate to maintain the privileg-

---

89 Stephen Cole, *Hockey Night Fever: Mullets, Mayhem and the Game's Coming of Age in the 1970s* (Toronto, ON: Doubleday, 2015), 10.
90 Derek Sanderson with Kevin Shea, *Crossing The Line: The Outrageous Story of a Hockey Original* (Toronto, ON: HarperCollins Press, 2012).

ing of certain forms of masculine identity over others. It is non-controversial to say, nonviolent sporting practices replete with their softer masculine imagery tend to be less valued in male sports culture. When it comes to gender imagery, consider what comes to mind for you when you compare volleyball, tennis, badminton or golf to hockey, football or rugby. Set against the backdrop of the social privilege afforded hockey players, not surprisingly, many young boys raised in contemporary Canada rarely fantasize about becoming a figure skater or a synchronized swimmer or a badminton player, in part because a boy who figure skates or becomes a synchronized swimmer is likely to be viewed by other boys as a 'sissy,' or assumed to be gay. For instance, the stereotype of the gay male figure skater conveys the message to men and boys that this form of identity is subordinate to the more revered kind of masculinity produced through hyper-aggressive sport such as ice hockey.[91]

So, it is clear that the legitimacy of men's ice hockey as a violent sport stands in opposition to less aggressive and thus less 'manly' sports.[92] Not surprisingly then, those men who have achieved success by playing professional hockey are often the most popular and admired people in the national context. In Canada, for example, and taking into consideration the privilege and benefit bestowed on men through the project of whiteness, we need only consider the enormous and widespread cultural and social status afforded to professional hockey players such as Bobby Orr and Wayne Gretzky to see the truth behind this statement. Keep in mind, that the new multimillion-dollar international bridge that is be-

---

91 For a detailed, historical discussion on the gendering of figure skating in North America, see Mary Louise Adams, *Artistic Impressions: Figure Skating, Masculinity, and the Limits of Sport* (Toronto: University of Toronto Press, 2011). It is also interesting that even between and among traditional acceptable male sports there is a hierarchy. The late comedian George Carlin once remarked on the difference between the rugged and manly sport of football and the less than masculine sport of baseball. "Football is played on a gridiron, baseball is played in a park . . . football players wear helmets, baseball players wear caps." See, Bruce Penton, "Rough Start for CFL Quarterbacks," *The Brooks Bulletin,* July 21, 2015, B6.

92 Of course, it also stands in opposition to women's athletics in general. According to a former collegiate basketball coach and athletic director at the University of North Carolina, "from high school to professional sports, female athletes are disadvantaged by a power structure dominated by men. The hierarchy of sports organizations, from state-level associations all the way up to worldwide organizations such as FIFA and the International Olympic Committee, consistently prioritizes the experience and needs of male athletes and the visibility of men's events." See, Helen Carroll, "Sexism, Homophobia Pervasive in Pro Sports," *Winnipeg Free Press,* June 27, 2015.

ing constructed between Windsor, Ontario and Detroit, Michigan will be named after well-known hockey player Gordie Howe, once again drawing our attention to the conflation of our national identity with a particular white hockey masculinity.[93]

Children and adults alike also learn through the context of elite male hockey that men who are unwilling to fight, find themselves labeled 'pansy,' or, 'fag,' or 'queer,' or 'sissy,' by their coaches, teammates and-or fans.[94] Men, after all are expected to be inherently aggressive and express a desire to fight, if need be. The fear of being viewed as a 'pansy,' 'sissy,' or 'queer,' is a powerful fear that often pushes men into fighting other men, dominates the most valued and accepted cultural definition of an 'appropriate' hockey masculinity. On March 8, 2004 in a game between the Vancouver Canucks and the Colorado Avalanche, Canuck player Todd Bertuzzi, late in the third period, went over the boards onto the ice to start a fight with Colorado player Steve Moore. In order to start a fight, Todd Bertuzzi employed homophobic and misogynistic slurs by calling him a "fuc--ng p--sy."[95] Bertuzzi ended up punching Moore from behind, in the back of the head, and landing on him, breaking Moore's neck and ending his hockey career. Even raising the question about limiting or outlawing hockey fighting triggers homophobic discourse. In January 2009, Mike Milbury, a former professional hockey player and coach with the Boston Bruins and once a well-known commentator for the Canadian Broadcast Corporation's (CBC) popular show, *Hockey Night in Canada*, for example, complained that the NHL has experienced a "pansification."[96] Milbury coined the expression to describe how the NHL would be 'feminized' should the NHL heed calls by a variety of groups to ban fighting from the game. Invested with homophobic and misogynist sentiments, Milbury's coining and public use of the term 'pansification' calls atten-

---

93 Dave Battagello, "Authority Holds First Public Meeting on Howe Bridge," *Windsor Star*, February 12, 2016, A3.

94 Former New York Islander superstar, Mike Bossy, wrote an article for *Inside Sports Magazine* in early 1980 when he was a player. In the article he told readers he "vowed not to fight." The article appeared two days before the 1980 Stanley Cup finals, which saw the New York Islanders play the Philadelphia Flyers. According to Bossy, fueled by his public declaration not to fight, Philadelphia fans "leaned over the glass" and repeatedly called him "faggot" during the warm up. See, Mike Bossy, *The Mike Bossy Story* (Toronto, ON: McGraw-Hill Ryerson, 1988), 119.

95 Alfred C. Davenport, Official Examiner, Toronto, Ontario, *Moore v. Bertuzzi*, Examination for Discovery.

96 W. Houston, "Gay Group Outraged by CBC's Use of Pansification," *Globe and Mail*, January 29, 2009, S1.

tion to how hockey has long been connected with hyper-masculine het-ero-normative versions of masculinity and implicated in the promotion and reproduction of homophobia.[97]

Milbury did it again. In 2011 Milbury called pro-hockey players and brothers, Daniel and Henrik Sedin, 'Thelma and Louise.' Daniel Sedin replied to Milbury's comment this way: "we don't really worry about those kind of comments. He made a bad comment about us, calling us women. I don't know how he looks at women. I would be pretty mad if I was a woman."[98] Although perhaps lessening to a very small degree, as people within the professional hockey community speak out against homophobia such as Brian Burke, whose son, Patrick Burke helped es-tablish the *You Can Play Project*, which seeks to eliminate homophobia in sport, and outspoken professional player Sean Avery[99] who appears to be a gay-straight ally, hetero-normativity and homophobia remain key factors in the definition of a hockey-masculinity. The hyper-masculinity that has shaped, and continues to shape hockey culture, makes it ex-tremely difficult for a player to come out.[100] In the NHL, there has yet to be a player who identifies as gay come out publicly, unlike in other professional sports organizations like the NBA or the NFL where play-ers such as Jason Collins (NBA), Michael Sam (NFL), and David Copey (NFL) have broken the boundaries.[101]

The very real and brutal world of hockey in which men continually act in hyper-competitive and aggressive ways often leads to their bodies be-

---

97 See, Brian Pronger, *The Arena of Masculinity: Sports, Homosexuality and the Meaning of Sex* (Toronto, ON: University of Toronto Press, 1992).

98 Eric Duhatschek, "Canucks' Sedin Brothers Rebuff Mike Milbury After Thelma and Louise Jab," *Globe and Mail,* June 11, 2011, S2.

99 In a 2011 interview with the *Toronto Sun,* Sean Avery said this: "if there is a kid in Canada or wherever, who is playing and really loves the game and want to keep playing but he's worried about coming out, I tell him to pick up the phone and call Donald Fehr (NHLPA Executive Director), and tell him to book me a plane ticket . . . I'll stand beside him in the dressing room while he tells his teammates he is gay. Maybe when Sean Avery is there, they would have less of a problem with it." See, Chris Stevenson, "Avery Would Support a Gay Player," *Toronto Sun*, February 3, 2011.

100 In the first international study on homophobia in sport, released in May 2015, it was found that the overwhelming majority, 73% of study-participants, believed that youth sport is not safe and wel-coming for lesbian and gay and bisexual people. The report went on to conclude that most gay men felt unwelcomed in sport with over 54% say they are not at all accepted. See, E. Denison, *Out On the Fields: The First International Study on Homophobia in Sport*, 2015.

101 Perhaps contrary to popular opinion, there are gay professional hockey players. For example, Eric Anderson reports that one of the "closeted professional" athletes that he interviewed for his research study told him he "met at least 11 other professional gay hockey players in his career." See, Eric Anderson, *In The Game: Gay Athletes and the Cult of Masculinity* (New York, NY: SUNY Press, 2005), 15.

ing exploited and abused in the training and medication process. Players from the NHL are expected to play often at the expense of their own health. Told to suck it up, man up, or stop being a pussy, the players do as they are told. Here is Fleury describing the relationship between gender expectations, men's bodies and the labour that was required of him by an internalized masculine ideology as a professional player:

> [T]here were times I was barely able to walk into the rink–ankle, shoulder, knee, concussion–but I was too proud. I could count on one hand the times I said I was injured, even then I still heard it - - 'Get out there. Suck it up'. [102]

Men's own fears of being considered unmanly push them to make decisions that work against the best interest of their health and welfare.[103] Consider the experiences of Rick Williams who was on the receiving end of numerous blows to the head during his hockey career as a junior in the Western Canadian League. Now 60 years old, and suffering from dementia, Williams identifies the repeated blows to the head during his hockey career as the source of his current health problems. For instance, he recalls returning to play in a game one day after coping with severe headaches caused by hit to the head during a previous hockey game. According to his father, Butch, his son Rick returned to play the game because he didn't want to be considered among his teammates and coaches as a "sissy."[104] Or consider, Derek Sanderson's experiences attending training camp in Niagara Falls in the fall of 1962. Here is Sanderson, "[f]or two days we scrimmage nonstop. Everybody was out to impress. If you carried it about 15 feet, you are really doing something special, and then boom! Somebody would run you over. You bleed, spit your teeth out and kept going, and the management in the stands would put a checkmark beside your name" ... 'that kid's got some balls.' That was old-school

---

102 Fleury, *Playing with Fire*, 104.
103 It is not just hockey, of course. Shea Emry, a professional football player who plays in the Canadian Football League recently said, "the culture of masculinity needs to change, so men can feel comfortable speaking their mind and not being criticized for having emotions and feelings." Emery goes on to note that for male professional athletes it is hard to express emotion in particular in all male spaces: "It's an alpha-male locker room where peacocking is non-stop" he said. See, Kevin Mitchell, "Emry Encourages Talking the Talk," *Leader Post* May 7, 2015, C1.
104 D. Nugent-Bowman, "Lessons to be Learned from Williams's Poor Health," [Saskatoon] *Star-Phoenix*, April 30, 2014, B2.

hockey. Courage was supreme." As Sanderson's comment suggests, for well over five of more decades within the contours of Canadian hockey culture a player must be willing to do anything to be noticed: A broken bone can heal over time; a cut can be stitched, a pulled muscle will eventually heal. And, missing teeth become a badge of honour among hockey players.[105] In the minds of many boys and men, physical and mental pain means nothing in the pursuit of a puck, a rite of passage for many Canadian boys.

Professional hockey inevitably leads to physical injury. Injury has been, and always will be part and parcel of the game. Consider the inevitability of physical injury: you put 12 hyper-competitive men (2 goalies, 10 skaters) on a clean sheet of hard ice 200 feet long and only 85 feet wide, who race around the rink on steel blades sometimes at speeds reaching 32 km an hour, continually colliding and hitting one another. It is a recipe for violence, one that may come as a surprise to those who are not familiar with the game. Here, for example, is Noble Prize novelist William Faulkner writing in the January 1955 issue of *Sports Illustrated*, discussing for readers his first impression of a professional hockey game, making special note of its inherent violence: "Excitement: man in rapid, hard, closed physical conflict, not just with bare hands, but armed with the knife blades of skates and the hard, fast, deft sticks which could break bones when used right." Faulkner goes on to mention what this means for little boys, "there must have been little boys in that throng too, frantic with the slow excruciating passage of time, panting for the hour when they would be Richard or Geoffrion or Laprade."[106] Put these facts alongside the gender expectation that not only men endure pain in silence, but you also end up with many players who voluntarily continue

---

105 Former professional hockey player and enforcer Tie Domi recently described for readers in his autobiography how he decided to "knock out" his two front teeth as a 12-year-old boy in order to look more like 1970s Philadelphia Flyers star Bobby Clarke. See, Tie Domi with Jim Lang, *Shift Work* (Toronto, ON: Simon & Schuster Canada, 2015), 20. Dr. Rick Lawson, the team dentist for the Phoenix Coyotes mentioned that in the context of professional hockey it was a "macho thing" to be missing teeth. He went on to mention that players receive an enormous amount of positive reinforcement from fellow players in the locker room, and others, who assume that the player must be tough because he's missing so many teeth. See, Joe Lapointe, "Hockey's Gap-Toothed Grin Fades Into The Past," *New York Times*, January 14, 2004. Larry Lage, writing recently in the *Globe and Mail*, noted that "[m]issing teeth have been associated with hard-nosed hockey-for better and for worse-for decades, becoming a stereotype of the game even with some players ... embracing it as a rite of passage or badge of honour." See, Larry Lage, "Grin and Bear It," *Globe and Mail*, February 10, 2016.
106 William Faulkner, "An Innocent at Rinkside," *Sports Illustrated,* January 24, 1955, 15.

to play after sustaining an injury. By sending this message, you produce powerful male role models who perpetuate an unhealthy lifestyle to boys who aspire to live up to the standards set out by the prevailing model of masculinity.[107] Boys want to fit in. But such potentially health compromising attitudes are clearly an issue, if this is what fitting in means.

Violent sports that promote a disregard for men's health help reinforce the gendered expectations found in the prevailing model of a so-called appropriate hockey masculinity. But these gender practices also need to be understood as set in the context that the professional hockey rink is an all-male space which links it closely to patriarchy. In these all male spaces, men (and boys) prove their superiority as a group because it is their bodies, not women's, which are capable of all that elite and professional hockey demands. But of course patriarchy isn't just about men dominating women, but also about men dominating other men. The inter-male dominance that defines elite and professional hockey, where one team of men conquers another team of men, and men compete with one another to be the strongest, fastest, toughest, makes hockey a key site for patriarchal practice.

Within Canadian male hockey culture, sexism and misogyny are pervasive. For example, in 2014, a popular web site called Junior Hockey Bible was shut down. The website was "essentially a sexual assault handbook for [male] hockey players and a celebratory rape culture manifesto" and revealed the misogynistic, sexist culture that underlies junior hockey.[108] Laura Robinson's work, *Crossing the Line: Violence and Sexual Assault in Canada's National Sport*, documents in some detail how Canadian Junior players are socialized in a way that sexual assault against women and girls is normalized. Robinson found that what boys really learn in junior hockey, to be understood as sort of hockey's hidden curriculum, is how to be misogynistic, sexist and violent.[109] The suspension of the men's hockey

---

107 It is not hard to see how hockey cards have been one vehicle to rationalize male violence and valourize male players who expose themselves to physical harm. For example, when a boy read the small blurb on the back of Buffalo Sabres' defenseman Jim Schoenfeld's 1977 Topps hockey card, he would have come across the following text: Jim Schoenfeld, who was named, "Sabres captain at the age of 22 . . . Played 8 playoff games in 1976 after suffering a broken foot."

108 Brendan Kennedy, "OHL Suspends Two Players for Sexist Online Conversation," *The Guelph Mercury*, November 7, 2014, B3.

109 Laura Robinson, *Crossing The Line: Violence and Sexual Assault in Canada's National Sport* (Toronto, ON: McClelland & Stewart, 1998).

program at the University of Ottawa in 2014 due to sexual assault allegations is one more example that reflects the deeply problematic nature of hockey culture when it comes to gender relations.

The belief that women are merely objects and available to hockey players to accumulate is also reflected in popular hockey related autobiographies. Here is former Calgary Flames player, Theo Fleury describing for readers, hockey players' attitudes toward women:

> A lot of hockey players have a different view of women then the rest of the world . . . [w]rong as it is, hockey players view women like cars. You have your own car and you love your car and you want to take care of your car, and you want to take your car to every important meeting you have, and you want it to be beautiful and shiny andsometimes with new headlights. But you love other guy's cars. You don't want to have their cars, but you would love to take them for a drive once in a while.[110]

If we take Fleury's testimony at face value, then in many ways, men's professional hockey is a place where relationships become sort of a game, with women as game pieces or rewards or conquests to be won after successful pursuit. The distorted and upside down moral code that regulates some men's behaviour in the hockey world as described by Fleury is not only defined by the way in which men are unable to trust other men, but also a distorted moral universe where the objectification, subordination and manipulation of women by men is rendered the norm.[111]

An idealized model of an 'appropriate' hockey masculinity is also invariably white. To be sure, whiteness has been for some time now been conflated with a hockey masculinity in such a way that it produces powerful and insidious forms of racism for non-white players. 1970s superstar Reggie Leach, who is of Métis background, was used to being called

---

110 Fleury, *Playing with Fire*, 209.
111 The professional men's hockey community largely considered 'hockey wives' as second-class citizens. Here is Dave Shultz explaining about gender relations and his experiences with the Philadelphia Flyers: "there were . . . players who felt that a woman belonged in the house and should be at the beck and call of her husband. They felt that a wife should go only where her husband permitted. It's a caste system: hockey wives are not considered to be in our class. Most players, coaches, and managers would like them to be-and considered them-subservient." See Shultz, *The Hammer*, 51.

a "dirty Indian" well before he turned professional.[112] Similar to Indigenous hockey players, black hockey players also grew up facing hockey related racism. Former NHL player Valmore James, for instance, recalls his difficult experiences as a black hockey player in his autobiography, *Black Ice: The Val James Story*. Here is James:

> When I started skating, I set out to be a hockey player, not a black hockey player. However, the two concepts quickly became intertwined. And not by choice. Early on, there were some people who are determinedto prove that being black and being a hockey player were mutually exclusive.[113]

Or consider the following example. In March 2003, former NHL goalie John Vanbiesbrouck, then the coach and general manager of the Ontario Hockey League's Sault Ste. Marie Greyhounds called team captain Trevor Daley a "ni- - er" in front of other members of the team. Shortly after the incident, Daley quit the team and Vanbiesbrouck resigned.[114] Back in 2011 playing in front of a crowd in London, Ontario, Philadelphia Flyers forward Wayne Simmonds, who is black, had a banana thrown at him during the pregame warm-ups. While the incident was widely denounced by hockey authorities and others, it does reflect the ongoing way in which hockey culture and communities are shaped by race and racism.

In some cases, men's experiences with racism resulted in a paradox, where their experiences as a player were structured in a way that out of the hockey rink they could be very popular and surrounded by friends and feel very little racism, but as soon as they were in the rink it became visible, explicit and palpable. Here is Georges Laraque – a former NHL player – describing his experiences growing up in Montreal:

> Throughout my childhood and teenage years, I experienced a big paradox in my relationships with others. As much as I was the victim of the most odious racism when I put on my skates in an arena, outside

112 Reggie Leach, *The Riverton Rifle: My Story-Straight Shooting on Hockey and on Life* (Vancouver, BC: Greystone Books, 2015).

113 Valmore James with John Gallagher, *Black Ice: The Val James Story* (Toronto, ON: ECW Press, 2015), 23.

114 "Game Misconduct," *Calgary Herald*, May 3, 2014, D2.

that 'environment I was very popular and surrounded by friends
... racism wasn't totally absent from my everyday life, but it remained a rare thing ... but racism isn't made up of only demon-
strable actions; it can be a lot more insidious. Let's take my hockey
years at Sorel-Tracy, for instance. Every single season, I was one
of the best players in my age group, yet I was never chosen to
play with the intercity team. My whole family, including me, knew
the reason for that.[115]

More recently, born of Caribbean parents, player P. K. Subban, who was
recently traded by the Montréal Canadiens to the Nashville Predators,
reminded people that even superstar hockey players, who embody many
of the characteristics of a dominant model of masculinity, are still subjected to various forms of racism. In 2014 after scoring the winning goal
in a heated double overtime playoff game against the Boston Bruins,
he was immediately subjected to racist comments.[116] Or consider the
example of New York Islanders' first round draft pick from the summer
of 2014, Josh Ho-Sang. Ho-Sang's father is Jamaican and his mother is
of Chilean Jewish decent, and his great grandfather was born in Hong
Kong. Ho-Sang related to the popular press that when he started 'dan-
gling' the puck his general manager called him a Harlem Globetrot-
ter.[117] Why draw the analogy to the famous basketball team, the Harlem
Globetrotters? Oddly, Ho–Sang mentions that analogies to basketball
are applied to him with some frequency, despite the fact that he doesn't
play basketball and has never played basketball. John Harris Jr., the first
black head coach in the history of professional hockey, faced a significant
degree of racism and hostility. He recalled having coins thrown at him,
one fan spit in his face, while others hung him in effigy from the raf-
ters of the rink with "the sign that had the N-word." He also goes on to
state that, during his coaching career, he received race-based hate mail
and death threats.[118] The overlapping of race and gender has produced

115 Georges Laraque with Pierre Thibeault, *Georges Laraque: The Story of the NHL's Unlikeliest Tough Guy* (Toronto, ON: Viking Canada, 2011), 32-35.
116 Sean Gordon, "P. K. Subban Not Fazed by Classless Acts of Sportsmanship," *Globe and Mail,* May 2, 2014, S2.

117 Bob Duff, "Ho-Sang Clears Air About Rychel Comments," *Windsor Star,* June 25, 2014.
118 Allan Maki, "Trailblazer Paris Jr. Would like to See More Black Coaches and Executives," *Globe and Mail,* June 28, 2013, S5.

a particular model of masculinity that functions to uphold inequalities based on race, a model of masculinity that has deep implications for those in hockey communities concerned with access and opportunities for all children to play the game.

It is also important to remember, there is a particularly strong relationship among hegemonic masculinity, sport, and capitalism, in particular corporate capitalism. Corporate capitalism has historically exploited the bodies of men and women in its pursuit of greater profit.[119] The promotion of a so-called ideal masculinity needs to be understood then, as closely connected to the interests of those men well positioned within the corporate capitalist structure. Take for example the testimony of Mike Peluso, who played ten seasons in the NHL for the Chicago Blackhawks, Ottawa Senators, among other teams. Currently, Peluso is struggling with serious health issues such as daily headaches and anxiety, memory loss and depression and at times, seizures. These long-term disorders, including early on-set dementia are likely the result of too many concussions. Peluso, while taking some personal responsibility has also expressed how male athletes have acquiesced so easily to the demands made by corporate capitalists. Here is Peluso:

> All we wanted to do was play, so we did whatever the NHL told us to do to stay in the game. We gave the NHL everything we had, and foolishly believed they had our best interests at heart. They failed to take care of us when we gave our blood and sweat to the game. [120]

Corporate capitalism teaches men such as Mike Peluso to develop a 'warrior' identity that is closely associated with physical toughness, competition, and public displays of bodily power. The business of the game

---

119 Maurice 'The Rocket' Richard, perhaps one of the most famous hockey players of all time, was by his fifties a "bitter" man. Richard's bitterness and resentment was directed at owners who made enormous amounts of money off his talent while treating him as a "slave." See, Robert Miller, "Newsy to Rocket to Guy," *Maclean's* April 5, 1976, 28-33. More recently, Sam Berg, a former junior player in the Ontario Hockey League (OHL), became the representative plaintiff in a class-action suit against the Canadian Hockey League (CHL). The primary concern of the suit rests on the poor working conditions players labour, in particular the way some team owners are making significant profits from the unpaid labour of the players. See, Nicholas Hune-Brown, "Hockey's Puppy Mill: A Former Junior Player Takes the CHL to Court," *The Walrus*, December 2015.
120 Mike Peluso, "The Game is Over, But the Suffering Has Only Begun," *Globe and Mail*, April 25, 2015, S1.

depends on these attitudes. Toronto Maple Leafs player Gary Leeman, who retired due to a series of significant injuries, noted how in his own playing days the "warrior mentality" was used to push players "to play through brutal injuries." Leeman notes that during one of his more serious head injuries, in which his skull was crushed, "he continually felt pressure [from coaches and owners] to put his health on the line and keep playing." But, the 'warrior mentality' is not just about pushing men to play at the expense of their own health, it also functions to keep men silent, despite their physical and physic pain. Once again here is Leeman: "I dealt with a lot of things in silence for a number of years ... I wasn't really prepared to speak to people in the game about it because I was considered to be a warrior. And if I told anybody about my issues, I felt like I was going to possibly lose my job."[121] Leeman's account reveals how his experiences were structured by the norms of a hyper-warrior masculinity and its adherence to a code of silence, at the same time shows how the masculine attributes that are closely associated with a professional hockey player's hegemonic masculine status, sacrificing one's body in silence for the sake of sporting glory remains significant.

But Leeman's testimony also demonstrates how men are willing to sacrifice their own health and welfare in order to keep their job. The testimony of former NHL player and hockey enforcer Ryan VandenBussche, who estimates that he suffered from at least a dozen concussions, puts this point into sharp relief:

> I hid my concussions ... I masked them with other injuries. I'm not a huge guy, by no means, but I fought all the big guys. And I certainly didn't want to be known as being concussion prone, especially early in my career, because general managers are pretty smart and your lifespan in the NHL wouldn't be very long.[122]

When it comes to major sporting leagues such as the National Hockey League (also the NFL), corporate capitalist structures encourage boys

---

[121] James Mirtle, "Former Leafs Star Gary Leeman Leads Retired NHL Players' Fight in Concussion Lawsuit," *Globe and Mail*, September 16, 2015, S1.
[122] John Branch, "Punched Out: The Life and Death of a Hockey Enforcer," in *The Best American Sports Writing*, edited by Glenn Stout (New York, NY: Houghton Mifflin Harcourt, 2012), 71-111.

and men to live up to the ideals of hegemonic masculinity by offering them exceptional material rewards, wealth, widespread adoration and fame and masculine honour. To play in the NHL almost guarantees a man his place among the so-called masculine elite in Canadian society. Yet keep in mind that by aspiring to live up to the ideals of hegemonic masculinity within the context of Canadian sport, men and boys routinely sacrifice their bodies and minds, including possibly experiencing depression, substance abuse, and premature death, all in the name of increasing corporate profits. One only has to consider the growing list of hockey enforcers who have recently died prematurely to see the hard truth of the matter: Bob Probert, Todd Ewen, John Kordic, Rick Rypien, Derek Boogaard, Wade Belak and Steve Montador. It has long been known that bodies are considered to be disposable and quickly discarded if they no longer serve the interests of capitalism, but the worrisome trend is particularly gaining notice in the context of professional hockey as enforcers continue to die prematurely.

The principle of profit over people, also forces hockey players to exchange brain cells for money, to put the matter crudely. The recent research on cognitive disease among hockey players is providing a deep evidentiary base that men who have a history of fighting are at significant cognitive risk. This is particularly true for those players who work, or did work, as enforcers. An enforcer's primary responsibility is to act in hyper-aggressive, hyper-violent ways and inflict harm on other players. This often means engaging in violent physical confrontations, fistfights, of which the consequences for a man's health can be significant. John Branch's work has chronicled the life of the former NHL hockey enforcer.[123] Branch details for the reader how Boogaard turned from a relatively shy, awkward and thoughtful teenager, who had very little interest in fighting, into one of the NHL's preeminent enforcers.[124] By putting his body and mind at risk each time he went out to play, he began showing signs of dementia. In his attempt to cope with the psychological and physical pain suffered on the ice, Boogaard became addicted to painkillers, drugs and abused alcohol. He died of an accidental overdose at the

---

[123] Branch, "Punched Out," 94.
[124] For a scholarly discussion on how the NHL exploits hockey enforcers see, Melanie Romero, "Check to the Head: The Tragic Death of NHL Enforcer Derek Boogaard and the NHL's Negligence – How Enforcers Are Treated as Second-Class Employees," *Jeffrey S. Moorad Sports Law Journal* 22 (2015): 270-303.

age of 28. The neuropathologists who examined his brain noted that they had never observed such deterioration in the brain of a person so young.

Although on the surface it rarely seems the case, men who labour away as enforcers rarely want to engage in repeated acts of violence on the ice. They certainly did not grow up playing hockey aspiring to be an enforcer. Who would? Here is former NHL enforcer, Brantt Myhres reflecting back on his experiences as a boy: "If you are playing pond hockey, six or seven years old, and somebody said, hey Brantt, the only way you're going to make it to the NHL is fighting your way there,' you think I would have done it? No way. I would have done something else."[125] Jamie Rivers, former teammate of deceased professional hockey enforcer Todd Ewen recalled that his friend [Ewen], "hated being a tough guy ... his whole career he hated it." So did former enforcer Dwight Schofield who started his hockey life as a "finesse player."[126] Former Montréal Canadian player Georges Laraque put the matter this way in his 2011 autobiography, *Georges Laraque: The Story of the NHL's Unlikeliest Tough Guy*:

> Every other tough guy in the league would rather do anything but fight on the ice. They would love to score tons of goals, become more and more talented, and earn bigger salaries, all the things hockey players dream of the moment they become hockey players. And I was one of those. I never enjoyed fighting. I did it because it was my job and the only way for me to keep playing in the NHL.[127]

Other hockey enforcers such as Chicago Black Hawks enforcer John Scott have also made statements about the significant amount of physical, emotional and psychological stress and anxiety that comes with the job. Here is Scott recalling the night before a typical game: "I had times where, going into a game, I know I'm going to get into a fight ... just the thought of getting into a fight, I just lay there, awake ... I'm nervous. I've got butterflies in my stomach. I'll probably get one hour of sleep.

---

125 Branch, *Punched Out*, 93.
126 Stan Fischler, *Bad Boys: The Legends of Hockey's Toughest, Meanest, Most Feared Players* (Toronto, ON: McGraw-Hill Ryerson, 1991), 88.
127 Laraque, *Georges Laraque*, 131.

It's exciting, nerve-racking, and terrifying all at the same time."[128] Of course, as was already mentioned, the failure to do the job puts one's employment at risk. For instance, former professional hockey player Paul Mulvey, when playing for the Los Angeles Kings during a game in 1982 was ordered out onto the ice by his coach, Don Perry with explicit orders to fight. At the time Mulvey was sitting on the bench. He disobeyed Perry's order and refused to go out on the ice. Attacking Mulvey's character and manhood, Perry accused him of being a coward and unwilling to defend his teammates. He then allegedly threatened Mulvey by saying he would never play professional hockey again. Mulvey was benched for the remainder of the game, and subsequently was exiled to the minor leagues where he would never resurface. By not adopting a blind willingness to live by the prevailing and powerful gender norms of the day, Mulvey's NHL career was over. For some players, fighting was the only way to keep their jobs.

Adhering to the 'pain principle' is key to establishing appropriate Canadian hockey masculinity. Briefly, the 'pain principle' states that a 'real' hockey player cannot openly admit to feeling physical, emotional or psychological pain.[129] The relationship between the pain principle and developing into a hockey player was noted over 40 years ago, in Gerald Eskenazi's 1972 book, *A Thinking Man's Guide to Pro Hockey*. Eskenazi noted that young Canadian boys who aspire to be a hockey player learn very young the kinds of values, attitudes and sacrifice needed to succeed in hockey. They learn at age 7 and 8 the physical demands of long seasons of 50 or 60 games; they learn the importance of physical and emotional

---

128 Branch, *Punched Out*, 94.

129 Don Sabo, "Pigskin, Patriarchy and Pain," *Changing Men: Issues in Gender, Sex and Politics, 16* (1986), 24-25. Other hyper masculine sports also promote a culture that is grounded in being tough and encourage men and boys to adhere to the pain principle. Here, for example, is one former professional football player describing his experiences which were guided by the pain principle and mixed in with misogyny: "I have been playing football since I was eight years old, and there is nothing more revered in football than being a tough guy . . . I prided myself on being a tough guy. I encouraged others to be tough guys. I did some horrendously stupid things in my career-like having surgery on Tuesday and playing on Sunday twice." He goes on to note that those men who did not play through pain and injury were routinely labeled "pussies." See, Mark Fainaru-Wada and Steve Fainaru, *League of Denial: The NFL, Concussions, and the Battle for Truth* (New York, NY: Crown Archetype, 2013), 80.

toughness, broken teeth, bruises, stitches, and pain.[130] Former professional hockey player, Barry Melrose put it this way in his 2012 autobiography *Dropping The Gloves*, "hockey players are a very macho group. You're judged by how tough you are, by how much pain you can take."[131] A so-called 'real' hockey player, then, learns early in life to accept the demands for player toughness and is expected to play through the pain. Dave King, former coach of the Montréal Canadiens, was very clear on what counts in hockey: "pain is one of hockey's measuring sticks." Former professional hockey player Jamie Rivers recalled his own experiences with the pain principle, stating that "we were programmed to not show pain from a young age ... your dad would tell you, 'Unless your dead, don't lay on the ice'."[132] In elite men's hockey, there is simply no so-called 'sissy stuff' allowed. A professional hockey player, must sacrifice their body for the team and those who fail to play due to injuries sometimes severe concussions, raise questions about their masculine character, their manhood. The failure to adhere to the pain principle, a key requirement in displaying an 'appropriate' Canadian hockey masculinity, triggers misogynist and homophobic slurs. For example, Sidney Crosby, a professional hockey player widely considered to be one of the best players in the world, has been called 'Cindy' in online environments. The labeling of Crosby as 'Cindy' has come about because his playing style and behaviour fails to conform to the so-called tough guy ideal of masculinity. This was particularly true after he suffered a severe concussion following hits to the head in back-to-back games during 2010-2011 season. Away from the line-up for just under a year, he was called a 'wimp' and needed to 'man-up'. Unfortunately, the close adherence to the pain principle by players has had a harmful influence on the attitudes of young players. A CTV news report in 2011 titled *Skull and Crosschecks,* for instance, reported that "self denial, the desire to be tough, to play through the pain, is something that junior players imitated" from professionals.[133]

---

130 According to researcher Kristi Allain, in Canadian hockey, media work to both construct and reinforce the common sense ways the game should be played. These media celebrate notions of masculinity that privilege aggression; and violence; playing with pain; and a rough Canadian style of play, specifically in men's hockey.

131 Melrose, *Dropping The Gloves*, 99.

132 James Mirtle, "Why Did Todd Ewen Lose the Fight of His Life," *Globe and Mail,* November 29, 2015, 1, 8-9.

133 CTV News, *Special Report: Skulls and Crosschecks* (Montreal, 2011). Available at montreal.ctvnews. ca

Conclusion

Hockey continues to be a key social institution in the making of Canadian masculinities. Professional hockey remains a place of male dominance, where men and boys live out the fantasy of assumed male superiority and rugged toughness, even though the majority of men and boys cannot play at the level of professional athletes. Male hockey cultures and communities remain key sites where boys learn to devalue and objectify women and girls, and engage in sexist practices. While it does appear to be lessening, homophobia remains one of the key ingredients in male hockey communities and cultures. Unfortunately, some boys also learn through organized hockey to hide and repress their emotional and physical pain in order not to show perceived weakness, making hockey a dangerous place for some boys. Not only does this flatten and narrow boys' lives and perhaps come at the cost of the development of their emotional life, but also the expectation to play through pain can be a source of long-term physical harm as the recent research on CTE as demonstrated. Finally, although sexism and homophobia are counter-productive lessons some boys internalize through hockey cultures and communities, and through the way that men and boys expose their bodies to physical risk, play while injured, and rehabilitate in order to be potentially injured again, it is clear that while men and boys may not actually enjoy physical violence and certainly not pain, the social, cultural and economic rewards afforded to those who aspire to the prevailing model of an 'appropriate' hockey masculinity remain significant.

CHAPTER THREE:
The Yellow Brick Road

C anadian literature, media and mythology are filled with romantic stories of hockey players going from farm ponds to careers in the National Hockey League (NHL). Even today, journalists and sport critics often debate the need for more 'fun' in hockey. Literature abounds with references to how 'hockey is being ruined by big business', or that children's sports are 'too organized'. Was hockey less organized, 'more fun' in its golden years? Could players go from unorganized pond games to a professional career in the 1960s? Is this a romantic image of Canada's hockey elite, or is this memory based in reality for the majority of early hockey professionals? The road for elite hockey players in Canada is not quite so romantic today. Players do not, and cannot, succeed to a professional career from pond to rink. This chapter explores the two pathways for players: the romantic 'yellow brick road' and the road more often travelled.

The Yellow Brick Road to the Hockey Pond

Early Canadian winters, prior to indoor heating and refrigeration, were long, cold, and snowy. Sports that could be played on ice and snow, like hockey, evolved out of those conditions. Finding exercise and activity outdoors in the winter months was born out of a need to find things to do in the environment one was given. Snowballs, snow forts, skiing, ice fishing, ice skating, and hockey were all sports one could participate in during the winter months. Good creation stories often begin in nature and Canada's game of hockey was no different. Beginnings evolve and are enriched by the raconteurs who pass on the stories and legends of a culture, and in Canada, some of the nations best and most prolific authors have threaded a 'natural' vision of hockey through the country's literature, and in turn, its culture. Two or three key Canadian authors immortalized the 'outdoor game' in *apriori* Canadian literature.

Literati Margaret Atwood's books are threaded with references to the Canadian environment and foundations set in the natural world. In her 1972 novel Survival, Atwood describes what it means to be essentially Canadian. This description of the 'Canadian experience' extends to hockey as well. Atwood said, "You could stay in your house, hibernate, wait for the thaw to come. But could we look ourselves in the national eye if we stayed indoors? Was there ever really any doubt that we'd get out and flood the yard and head out over the bridge to the pond?"[134]

Atwood claims that skating on an outdoor rink in the Winter *is* Canadian; that, to do otherwise, would be shameful. And prior to any form of indoor arenas or manufactured methods of freezing ice rinks, skating outdoors was the only option. It was the equivalent of hiking up a mountain to ski down prior to ski lifts. If you were Canadian, this was one of the sports you were expected to participate in during the winter months because to do otherwise would be weak and demeaning.

Former NHL player Duane Sutter recalls, "playing all night when the moon was full" at the pond north of Viking, Alberta[135]. And colder parts of the country, such as Ville de Québec and Ottawa had outdoor hockey rinks longer. "When the moon was full", like a candle-lit evening with a loved one, is a romantic, rustic scene. Many Canadian families have memories of early twentieth century winters and recreation outdoors. My own grandfather told this story about 1920s Ontario:

134 Stephen Smith, *Puckstruck: Distracted, Delighted and Distressed by Canada's Hockey Obsession* (Vancouver, BC: Greystone Books Ltd., 2014), 66.
135 Ibid., 44.

Early Saturday morning after our chores were done, we would each take a hot potato from the stove and wrap it in foil or a cloth, then put one in each skate. Then we would walk the two miles down the road to the nearest pond to meet up with the boys on the next farm. The potatoes kept our skates and shoes warm, and had the added benefit of providing lunch as well!

In Roch Carrier's timeless children's book, *The Hockey Sweater*, set in Ste.-Justine, Québec, the characters "lived in three places – the school, the church and the skating rink – but [their] real life was on the skating rink."[136] The characters in Carrier's book grow up pretending to be Montréal Canadiens' forward Maurice 'Rocket' Richard, all wearing the same hockey jersey on the ice. Many Canadian hockey families have read this book as children, and although it follows the life of a fan, not a professional player, the inference the reader is left with is that elite hockey players in Québec started playing outdoors. If your dream was to be a professional hockey player, then you began playing outdoors, on pond ice, in the country, copying other NHL greats.

In author Steven Galloway's secondary school novel, *Finney Walsh*, main characters Paul and Finnie (the mill owner's son) grow up in the early twentieth century playing on outdoor ice, each aspiring to and reaching elite hockey in the NHL.[137] The novel has a sacrificial, Christ-like ending when Paul's lifejacket-wearing sister correctly predicts Finnie's death-by-whistle at the game-winning goal. It is this humble, outdoor beginning on the pond ice of a gravel pit that see the characters Paul and Finnie through to the NHL—but it is also fiction.

Critic and former NHL player Jason Blake reviewed the works of over eight major Canadian writers, including Roch Carrier, Mordecai Richler, Alice Munro, and politicians Michael Ignatieff and Stephen Harper[138] and their protrayals of elite hockey players on outdoor, natural rinks in

---

136 Roch Carrier, *The Hockey Sweater, Montréal*, (PQ: Tundra Books, 1979).

137 Steven Galloway, *Finnie Walsh*, (Toronto, ON: KnopfRandomVintage Canada, 2000).

138 Stephen J. Harper, *A Great Game: The Forgotten Leafs and the Rise of Professional Hockey*, (Toronto, ON: Simon & Schuster Canada, 2013).

NEXT TO THE ICE

the middle of Canada's countryside(s). Each work enriches and expands this idea of classic hockey starting on ice rinks outdoors in the country.[139]

Author and sports columnist Dave Stubbs further enforces this image of national [outdoor] hockey in his book *Our Game*: "Before the NHL, in Canada, the game was first enjoyed on frozen ponds and rivers and was often called 'shinny', a word derived from the 17th Century Scottish game of 'shinty', or pick up hockey."[140]

Canadian authors and their characters all propagate a romantic image of Canada's hockey game learned in the 'great outdoors' of country farm ponds and small towns. And this probably was not far from the truth in early Canada. When the general population thinks of outdoor skating, it is a quiet, serene, pastoral setting that is conjured. As Buma demonstrates, the Canadian hockey landscape is continually mythologized through sports and fictional literature alike. "Our winters are typically rendered as pure pastoral settings, our frozen rivers and ponds and outdoor rinks as idealized Edens where the true Canadian [male] spirit finds its noblest, freest expression"[141] in hockey. Outdoor hockey is so integral to Canada's mythic beginnings that even the money, the former $5 Canadian bill, depicts an outdoor hockey rink with children playing in NHL jerseys.

Lord Frederick Stanley, the sixth Governor General of Canada and 16th Earl of Derby, was a close friend of Canada's first Prime Minister, Sir John A. MacDonald. Lord Stanley and his wife enjoyed outdoor hockey so much that they maintained an outdoor rink on their lawns at Rideau Hall. Having the Prime Minister's best mate, and Queen Victoria's own crown representative, endorse hockey helped to promote and secure the game's importance as a national past-time across the country. When the Governor General offered to donate a prize, the "Dominion Hockey Challenge Cup", to the best hockey team in the nation, the award quickly became known by the name it carries today, "The Stanley

---

139 Jason Blake, *Canadian Hockey Literature: A Thematic Study*, (Toronto, ON: University of Toronto Press, 2010).

140 Dave Stubbs, *Our Game: The History of Hockey in Canada* (Montréal, PQ: Lobster Press, 2006), 24.

141 Michael Buma, *Refereeing Identity: The Cultural Work of Canadian Hockey Novels*, (Kingston. ON: McGill-Queen's Press, 2015).

Cup."[142] Thus, from the highest, most aristocratic levels of government, and the widest breadth of Canadian literature, 'pure hockey' was played outdoors. Outdoor pond hockey was the place the 'true hockey player' learned the core of the craft.

Ergo, who actually played [elite] pond hockey? How many farmers went from 'the pond' to the NHL? Was this even a reality? The first, of-ficially-recorded, organized games of hockey in Canada were at the Mc-Gill University Club in 1881 and 1884, but it was not until New Year's, 1898, after Lord Stanley's cup, that the first match inside the Montréal Arena was held.

It is wistful to think of fresh air and country ponds organically produc-ing the strongest, best hockey players around, but the stark reality is that most elite hockey players develop their speed and skill through long daily hours of practice and skating in *indoor* rinks with scarce resources and ice time, not in the great outdoors. Most elite hockey athletes are an indoor gym and arena phenomena.

Oz is Indoors

Canada is the largest land mass in the World, with a comparatively small population per square kilometers. It is understandable then, with all that open land, the image of Canada's unofficial national game would be one of elite players honing their skills in the survival-like conditions of icy outdoor snow and sub-zero temperatures. Did this happen for the names we know best in hockey?

Let us begin with 'The Great One': Wayne Gretzky. Wayne's dad Wal-ter did grow up in the country, in a farming community, skating on the local river in winters with his brothers—but Wayne never did.[143] By the time Wayne was born, the Gretzky family were living in an apartment and then a small house in Brantford and, with the help of his father's time and coaching, Wayne developed his skills night after night on in-door rinks in Brantford and beyond.

---

142 Dave Stubbs, *Our Game: The History of Hockey in Canada* (Montréal, PQ: Lobster Press 2006,) 8.

143 Walter Gretzky, *On Family, Hockey and Healing,* (Toronto, ON: Random House, 2001).

Paul Kariya grew up in downtown Vancouver and played exclusively indoors from the age of three.[144] Jaromír Jagr grew up outside of the international city of Prague and played organized hockey in the capital until he emigrated for work in the NHL.[145] Eric Lindros played on a frozen urban backyard swimming pool from age 9-16 and played for organized teams inside rinks across the city.[146] Mario Lemieux *did* skate and play shinny on an outdoor rink in central Montréal, one of the city-owned public rinks for residents and visitors, while concurrently playing organized indoor hockey with the city's elite teams.[147]

Despite calls from Canadian Minor Hockey and its affiliates for "kids to have fun while playing,"[148] and despite the persistent Canadian image of an earlier, romantic countryside version of pastoral hockey, most elite players focused on a position in the NHL to work for hockey organizations as a profession, not play-work, and hard work.

For example, the Bobby Orr organization is one of the biggest proponents of 'kids having fun playing while they are young,' and 'keeping the business out of hockey', but "the same man who thinks young players should be left alone to play represented both Aaron Eckblad and Connor McDavid [at only ten years of age], and both were granted exceptional status to play in the OHL (Ontario Hockey League) at age 15."[149] Aaron Eckblad, Connor McDavid and John Tavares were obviously not skating around farm ponds in their childhood. By childhood, they already had a professional sports' agent and a full-time indoor schedule of hockey practices and developmental skill clinics. This represents a grand hypocrisy in the sport. Former NHL players, who themselves advocate for 'the enjoyment of the game' and keeping 'kids kids', also make the most profit out of clinics and camps and pushing 'elite hockey' early in a player's life, as early as age 10, 11- an age when most Canadians imagine young national players skating outdoors in the fresh air for fun.

---

144 Mike Bonner, *Paul Kariya* (Philadelphia, PA: Chelsea House Publishers, 1999), 15.

145 Dean Schabner, *Jaromir Jagr* (Philadelphia, PA: Chelsea House Publishers, 1997), 13.

146 John Kreiser, *Eric Lindros* (Philadelphia, PA: Chelsea House Publishers, 1997), 9-16.

147 Brian Tarcy, *Mario Lemieux* (Philadelphia, PA: Chelsea House Publishers, 1997), 15.

148 Paul M. Valliant, *Minor Hockey to NHL: Parents' Survival Guide* (Victoria, BC: Trafford Publishing, 2007), 40-42.

149 Ken Campbell with Jim Parcels, *Selling the Dream: How Hockey Parents and Their Kids Are Paying the Price for our National Obsession*, (Toronto, ON: Viking Press, 2013), 5.

Mitchell Davis, the seven-year-old wonder from North Bay, Ontario was scouted shortly after beating Wayne Gretzky's 'most goals scored by a seven-year-old' record during an elite year of travel hockey. His early career was demolished shortly after, however, by the media onslaught of his age seven 'professional career.'[150]

Derek Boogaard was placed into hockey programs in "chilly rinks" at age five and his parents spent all their free money on registration fees, equipment and tournaments.[151] A similar spiral occurred with the elite team and skill development of Mike Danton in organized hockey.[152] In such rinks where players are taught to network and the sport is politicized, it can be a breeding ground for deviant, even criminal, behaviour. Theo Fleury said, in his victim-impact statement of former convicted coach Graham James, "it was drilled into me that he held keys to making my dream a reality" (February 22, 2012). Those games and play were not 'fun'.

Players that do begin hockey late (that is, after age 6) are, on average, 100 hours per year behind other players in skills development. If the child plays travel or AAA hockey, those hours per year jump to 325 or more. In Malcolm Gladwell's *Outliers*, it is suggested that players reach the height of their career at 10,000-hours. *Ergo*, the more hours of ice time per week of practice a player receives, the more likely they are to hit that magic 10,000-hour mark.

Sheer hours in ice practice is not the only way to distinguish one's ability. Ericsson's study of elite violinists suggests that once a musician has enough ability to audition and get into a top music school, the only thing that distinguishes one performer from another is how hard they work.[153] In 2007, Guillermo Campitelli and Fernance Gobet found that some chess players reached 'master status' in 3,000 hours and some in 24,000.[154] It was the intensity and drive, not the hours, that made the

---

150 Ibid., 10.
151 John Branch, *Boy on Ice: The Life and Death of Derek Boogaard* (Toronto, ON: Harper Collins Publishers Ltd., 2014), 21-22.
152 Steve Simmons, *The Lost Dream: The Story of Mike Danton, David Frost and a Broken Canadian Family* (Toronto, ON: Viking Canada, 2011).
153 Ken Campbell with Jim Parcels, *Selling the Dream*, 2013, 117.
154 Ibid., 120.

difference in the level of play. When Brett Hull was asked what was the most important skill he got from his NHL father, he said, "genes."[155] Hence, if a child is going to develop into an elite hockey athlete in Canada, they will not need an outdoor pond in the country. They will need: parents to pass down the genetic athletic size and material to their children, and the time and money to give their children a head start in the 10,000-hour number game.

The monetary cost of elite hockey development, in itself, can be exclusionary for parents of exceptional athletes. The total cost of a Nepean (Ottawa) Raiders' Minor Atom (age 7), for example, is $8, 315.00 per year.[156] If travel (mileage), accommodation, food, equipment, and lost work hours are calculated into that figure, the cost is closer to $30,000 per year and that does not include clinics and development camps, run by ex-professionals at thousands of dollars.

Lindsay Hofford, for example, CEO of Pro Hockey Development Group, will evaluate players, teams, and hold tournaments for thousands of dollars.[157] In central Ontario, elite teams travel to the U.S.A. for tournaments run by professional corporations for thousands of dollars. Private hockey schools, such as the Hill Academy in Toronto, or the Okanagan Hockey Academy in Penticton, B.C., have been called, 'the Disneyland for hockey players;'[158] and the Harrington College of Canada in Montreal advertises, "where the serious hockey player goes to school."[159]

Most parents feel "duty bound to help their children realize their dreams,"[160] and as such, will invest both time and money to help them get there, whether it is into university or a good college; starting up their own business; or going into professional arts/sports careers.

In hockey, this projectory begins young, teaching children how to skate about the same time they are learning to walk. Learning to skate means weekly trips to the local ice rink during public or children's skating.

155 Ibid., 117.
156 Ibid., 103.
157 Ibid., 135.
158 Ibid., 148-150.
159 Ibid., 153.
160 Michel Roy, *Patrick Roy: Winning. Nothing Else* (Mississauga, ON: John Wiley & Sons Canada, Ltd., 2007), 41.

Then, parents enroll their children in house league 'tyke' hockey beginning at age 4, or before they enter kindergarten. Most tyke games are dominated by good skaters, and the skating is what gets a child noticed at age 4-5 prior to select travel teams in atom at age 7. Once a child tries out for, and makes, a travel team, their ice time and developmental practices at the rink doubles. They are then able to travel to play other skilled players in their region, racking up additional work hours of skill development, exposure, and on-ice play. AAA teams begin at age 8-9, and then ice time, or practice time available, and games per week, double again, and the season extends from August to the following May (approximately 8-9 months, including 'tryout season'). For those children entering hockey later, even at age 8 or 9, which is only grade 2-3, the number of hours and 'political clout' the child has already missed, like a child who enters school having never read a book, is possibly too much of a gap to ever catch up.

Learning to excel in a sport may be compared to a type of literacy. To excel in mathematics or writing or science, a student needs to study and work at the discipline. Exciting rewards come from conquering a skill. Elite athletes are no different. They may be developing different parts of their body and minds; however, the dedication and focus is similar. Discipline is required. Long hours of concentration must be maintained to master a concept and skill, and athletes, like students, must be capable of pleasing and working with mentors to move up.

'Political clout,' as most parents know, is an important part of early hockey. Negative [parental] behaviour in the arena can create problems for the child, and "a parent who is stigmatized as a 'gossip' or a 'rabble rouser' could follow the child from team to team" and even affect their ability to make key teams that provide more skill development.[161] The same is true of deviant behaviour in a school: that reputation may follow students regardless of ability. Coaches will not select minor hockey players onto their teams if their parent(s) have a reputation for poor behaviour.[162] Similarly, parents who are well-liked, fun, or get along well with a coach, are more likely to have their child – who might play at a

---

161 Paul M. Valliant, *Minor Hockey to NHL*, 2007, 36.
162 Ibid.

mediocre level – make an elite team. Those are the unwritten rules of the game.

Although elite hockey development in Canada is a stark contrast from the romantic mythology of the game the nation has built, the indoor game development is equivalent to any passionate pursuit. Hockey's Eden, Mecca, or Promised Land may be the romantic outdoor frozen ponds of our ancestors' fields, but every spiritual beginning must be born of an ideal. Otherwise, what is there to strive for? The Yellow Brick Road of Canadian hockey may lead to a disappointing reality, but along the way, it may also teach discipline, hard work, how to succeed from failure, and how to resiliently commit to the higher purpose of the group. The Yellow Brick Road may not be all fresh air and fun, but can one truly experience pleasure in life without genuine sacrifice and personal work?

CHAPTER FOUR:
Working Class Hero: Exploring the Rise of the 1970s Hockey Enforcer

Introduction

The role of the 'hockey enforcer' emerged in a new and unprecedented way during the 1970s. The rise of the enforcer during this era was fuelled by a number of complex historical factors including the National Hockey League (NHL) expansion in 1967 when the Original Six teams became 12; the lengthening of the NHL season from 70 to 78 games; and the emergence in late 1971 of a rival league, the World Hockey Association (WHA). These changes created a new demand for labour within professional hockey. Old teams and new teams were desperate for any kind of talent. So, players of less calibre such as the Plager brothers—Bob, Barclay and Bill were now finding playing opportunities to play at the professional level. It was also at this time that teams began to understand that rostering a tough guy could help win them games. Montréal Canadiens player, John Ferguson provided an early model for other teams during the 1960s, and is considered by some to be hockey's "original enforcer."[163] Put together, along with other factors the increased demand for hockey labour opened up many new opportunities

---

[163] Stan Fischler, *Bad Boys: Legends of Hockey's Toughest, Meanest, Most Feared Players* (Toronto, ON: McGraw Hill Ryerson, 1991), 80.

that were not previously available to players and rendered possible the ascendancy of the hockey enforcer.

In the 1970s, gender articulated with social class in the determination of who became a hockey 'enforcer.' The men who became enforcers in the 1970s were made enforcers by their class position, rather than by their natures. The enforcers were not born to violence, nor were they necessarily naturally inclined to fight. Rather, along with the pressures of adhering to a masculine ideology which normalized and valorized male violence, it was their class position growing up in working poor, working-class, often immigrant communities, that moulded them and fuelled their desire to do whatever it took to become a professional hockey player. Enforcers such as Jerry 'King Kong' Korab, Dave 'The Hammer' Shultz, Terry 'Bloody' O'Reilly, John Wensink, Dave 'Tiger' Williams, Steve 'Demolition Durby' Durbano and Bob Plager knew at a young age they literally had to fight their way out of a world that offered working class boys very few life chances. Hockey became a pathway to affluence and success.

But there is much more to the story of the rise of the 1970s hockey enforcer than this. Beginning in the early 1970s, the hockey enforcer came to hold a special appeal among the general public and many hockey fans. Throughout this period, hockey enforcers were promoted and popularized not only on the basis of whiteness but also on the basis of their perceived working-class nature, at a time when white working-class identities were in the words of then American president Richard Nixon "forgotten."[164] Within the American context, high profile enforcers from the 1970s such as Dave Shultz and John Wensink offered hockey fans and

---

164 Throughout the 1970s, the term and idea of the 'forgotten-man' was presented to the public as speaking for and the embodiment of 'traditional' values. In this sense, traditional values, which were best understood as --patriarchal, class-based, racist and hetero-normative-- were linked with white masculinity that escaped the perceived 'softness' thought to be pervading American culture in the wake of the so-called 'permissive' 1960s. For white working class men during the 1970s, it was an anxious time as they feared that 'normalcy' was being eroded by significant changes in society, including challenges by various groups of 'others' such as women, gays, non-white identities, who were, so they thought, threatening to invalidate the very terms of the very category that the forgotten-man would seemed to depend. The increasing presence of gays, lesbians and bisexuals in society, ran along side concerns over the breakdown of the nuclear family and the rise of female led households, which did very little to comfort those wedded to traditional notions of 'normalcy.' As such, white working and middle class men became constructed within popular and professional discourse as 'wounded,' 'weakened,' and 'vulnerable.'

others a symbol of the self-made man who embodied historically prized masculine values of strength, individualism, toughness, and determination, at a time when white working-class males were anxious and fearful that 'normalcy' was being undermined by large scale changes in society. The white hockey hero-enforcer, whose masculinity confirmed the values of patriarchy, the work ethic and rugged individualism, and who clearly demarcated the boundaries between men and women, black and white, became, if nothing more, a symbol, an expression, and an outlet for white male middle and working class anxieties and frustrations in the age of economic retrenchment.

Drawing on a wide range of materials including men's biographies and autobiographies, popular periodicals of the time such as The Canadian Magazine, Time, Maclean's, Newsweek, and *Sports Illustrated*; popular newspapers such as the *Globe and Mail* and *The Toronto Star*, and assorted hockey related materials such as Topps and O-Pee-Chee hockey trading cards, this chapter explores the emergence of the hockey enforcer in the 1970s. I highlight the key historical factors that led to the rise of the hockey enforcer in the 1970s, and then briefly explore the lives of a handful of enforcers of the time. Finally, in this chapter I also briefly bring to light the way in which the 1970s hockey enforcer became a rallying point for white male working-class identities who were challenged by large scale social, political and economic change within the American context. I conclude by arguing that the rise of the hockey enforcer was shaped by particular historical changes in the context of professional hockey, and its public reception and growing popularity was fuelled by social, economic and political challenges to traditional white male working class masculinity.

The Hockey Enforcer in the Pre-1970s Era

Although not considered hockey enforcers, there did exist various versions of the tough guy in professional hockey prior to the 1970s. 'Bad' Joe Hall in the 1910s and Billy Coutu in the 1920s quickly come to mind. In fact, Coutu became infamous after a 1927 incident where he punched a referee in the Stanley Cup final. He was subsequently suspended for life, only to be later reinstated. Red Horner in the 1930s and Reggie 'The Ruffian' Fleming in the 1960s are also well known tough guys during their own respective time periods. However, when discussing early tough guys, Montréal Canadiens player John Ferguson deserves special mention. Ferguson was added to Montréal's line up in the 1960s to protect more skilled players such as Jean Beliveau.[165] In the December 19, 1970 edition of *The Canadian Magazine,* writer John Zichmanis dubbed him the "original enforcer."[166] In large measure, Ferguson was recruited to offset teams such as the Chicago Blackhawks and the Toronto Maple Leafs who were beginning to acquire "mean players." These teams acquired so-called "mean players" in order to stop the high-flying, highly skilled Montréal Canadiens. Montréal's successful experiment with Ferguson as a deterrent to other teams at the end of the Original Six Era would contribute greatly a few years later to "both the number of enforcers in the NHL and their importance." [167]

It was common knowledge that Ferguson was not a skilled player. Here is writer Hanford Woods describing Ferguson precisely in this way in his 1988 short story, *The Drubbing of Neseterenko:*

> He [John Ferguson] was hardness itself, a face of rock-solid bone, a body of ungainly, awkward muscle. He had no style: he remains to this day the one hockey player who could lose a puck when no-one had challenged him for it. He would pick up a free puck, lose it in his skates, and, like a dog chasing its tail, whirl furiously, vainly seeking it. [168]

---

165 A player scout in the 1960s for the Montréal Canadiens, Scotty Bowman recalled in a recent interview that it was during the early 1960s, in particular the 1961 playoff series against a tough Chicago Blackhawks team, that motivated the Montréal Canadiens to recruit John Ferguson. Bowman recalled, "Chicago was full of big, strong guys like Reggie 'The Ruffian' Fleming and Murray Balfour," who prevented "the skilled players from not being able to exhibit the skill they had." In fact, Bowman recalled that at least three Canadiens – including John Beliveau – suffered concussions against that particular Chicago team during the series. See, Patrick White, "Down for the Count," *Globe and Mail,* March 21, 2015, S1.

166 John Zichmanis, "John Ferguson Likes Horse Racing Better Than Hockey," *The Canadian Magazine,* December 19, 1970, 24-27.

167 G. Oliver and R. Kamchen, *Don't Call Me Goon: Hockey's Greatest Enforcers, Gunslingers, and Bad Boys* (Toronto, ON: ECW Press, 2013), 61.

168 Hanford Woods, "The Drubbing of Neseterenko," in *The Rocket, The Flower, The Hammer and Me,* edited by Doug Beardsley (Winlaw, BC: Polestar Press, 1988), 237-262.

Ferguson did not require "style" as a player, he was mostly there to protect his team and intimidate others. This change in thinking in the post 1967 much-expanded National Hockey League, which ran alongside the emergence of the rival WHA, provided opportunities to those players who previously couldn't make a professional team. So, players of less calibre such as Ron Ward of the Cleveland Crusaders (WHA) were no longer cut from professional rosters.[169] "A lot more players have the opportunity to make it who may be weren't as skilled, but were tough or strong," noted former NHL player, Terry Harper discussing pro-hockey in the 1970s. Harper went on to note that, "there were tough guys when there were just six teams, but they couldn't get by just on toughness alone. I think after, there was a while there they could."[170] Certainly Harper was correct in that there were some very tough players in the pre-expansion era, but these players were also highly skilled. Players like Gordie Howe and Bobby Hull were more than willing to drop the gloves and fight if need be, but they were also very capable of being the scoring leaders of their respective teams, if not the league. To put differently, during the Original Six Era skilled players like Howe and Hull were much harder, if not impossible, to intimidate than many of the best players from the 1970s. Therefore, Original Six Era teams did not need to carry a designated enforcer to protect their stars. But this was to change by the early 1970s as the hockey enforcer became much more of a specialized role.

The 1970s

In the 1970s a hockey enforcer became a specialized, if not an unofficial, role in elite and professional ice hockey. It was a time, said one former player that "required teams to have guys on the roster who were there

---

169 On the back of Ron Ward's 1974 World Hockey Association's O-Pee-Chee hockey trading card he is described in a less than flattering way: "if there were no WHA, there's a good chance that Ron might not be playing major-league hockey today."
170 Oliver and Kamchen, *Don't Call Me Goon*, 61.

solely for fighting."[171] By the early 1970s, an enforcer's primary responsibility was to deter and respond to dirty or violent play by the opposition players. When such incidents occurred the enforcer was expected by his fans, teammates, and coaches to respond aggressively by dropping the gloves and fighting the offending player. More specifically, enforcers were expected to react particularly harsh to violence against their team's star players or goalies. In 1974 for example, enforcer Dave 'The Hammer' Shultz was dubbed "hockey's number one villain," by *The Sporting News*. Shultz played for the Philadelphia Flyers during their Stanley Cup years (1974 and 1975) and was primarily tasked to protect star players such as Reggie Leach and Bobby Clarke.[172] Well-known hockey columnist of the time, Stan Fischler, writing in the same March 16, 1974 issue of the *Sporting News* put the matter of Shultz in this straightforward way: "when Bobby [Clarke] is in trouble, the Dave Schultzs . . . do their number on other peoples heads."[173] Perhaps Larry Playfair, who began his career as an NHL enforcer in 1978 with the Buffalo Sabres, summed up in very explicit ways what his job was: "to protect the stars."[174] To be sure, as the 1970s progressed there was less and less ambiguity around the role of the enforcer. They were there to intimidate and strike fear into the hearts of opponents. And, according to Barry Melrose, a former player during the 1970s, "intimidation qualified as a game plan." [175]

During the 1970s, at the level of the professional hockey, teams generally did not carry more than one player whose primary role was an

---

171 Barry Melrose with Roger Vaughan, *Dropping The Gloves: Inside the Fiercely Combative World of Professional Hockey* (Toronto, ON: McClellan and Stewart), 195.

172 Although his job was to protect stars like Bobby Clarke, Shultz did not necessarily have much respect for Clarke as a player. Here is Shultz, "I watched many Flyers games and have seen many of his [Clarke] slashes, spearing, high-sticking and cross checking, but can't recall Clarke ever willing to stand man-to-man with his victim's attempt at just satisfaction. I'm glad he's on my hockey team, but I wouldn't have wanted him within one mile of me on Normandy Beach . . . In a sense I envy Clarke. Can you imagine what a unique situation he was in for a hockey player-knowing that he could do almost anything to the opposition and not have to worry about answering for himself since there were enforcers like me around to fight his battles?" See, Dave Shultz with Stan Fischler, *The Hammer: Confessions of a Hockey Enforcer* (New York, NY: Summit books, 1980), 118-119.

173 Stan Fischler, "Speaking Out on Hockey," *The Sporting News*, March 16, 1974, 4.

174 Oliver and Kamchen, *Don't Call Me Goon*, 144.

175 Although by the early 1970s hockey teams such as the Philadelphia Flyers made intimidation part of their game plan, it was the expansion team, the St. Louis Blues that started the trend, according to John Ferguson. Ferguson recalls that it was the three Plager brothers, Bob, Barclay and Bill, who became known as the Royal Family of Mayhem, who started the trend. See, Oliver and Kamchen, *Don't Call Me Goon*, 62.

enforcer. Enforcers played either forward or defense, although they were most frequently used as wingers. Like John Ferguson before him, Shultz, for example, played left wing, as did Toronto's Dave Williams. Boston's Terry O'Reilly played right wing. New York Islander's Clarke Gillies played on the left. Prized for their physical aggression, checking ability and fists, enforcers were typically less gifted in skill areas of the game such as puck handling and shooting than their teammates. Author Roy MacGregor, writing in the October 16, 1978 issue of *Maclean's* used a useful music analogy to compare the talents and skills of a popular 1970s enforcer to that of a much more skilled player, Montréal's high flying Guy Lafleur: "One of the Boston Bruins players, John Wensink['s] ... hockey talent is to [Guy] Lafleur's what punk rock is to Beethoven."[176]

Enforcers typically received a smaller share of ice time. The more skilled players received about 30 to 40 minutes of playing time a game, while an enforcer typically saw only a fraction of that. An NHL player from the 1970s explained: "every team picks up their tough guys ... guys just to fight ... they send them out to play about 10 minutes of the game, and their only job is to stir up trouble, start fights, and get the good guys off the ice"[177] However, there were exceptions to this rule. Players such as Bill Plett, Clarke Gillies, Dave Williams and John Wensink were not only fighters, but scorers as well, and saw a fair share of ice time. But in general enforcers were not thrown on the ice during a game to score goals.[178] They were there to win fights. An enforcer who lost fights, found himself without work. And, they were expected to get penalties and plenty of them. Not surprisingly then, they were often the penalty minute leaders of their respective teams, and during the 1970s set outrageous league records. Philadelphia Flyer player Dave Schultz, for example, still holds the all-time NHL record for penalty minutes for one season with 472 (1974-1975). As one of the NHL's toughest men,

---

176 Roy MacGregor, *Maclean's*, 46-52.
177 Melrose, *Dropping the Gloves*, 51.
178 Some enforcers wanted to improve their hockey skills in order to score goals, but were discouraged to do so by their teammates. For example, here is Dave Schultz explaining his teammates' reaction to his effort to improve himself as a skilled player: "Being the target of my teammates' ridicule was hardest to take. They would constantly mock my efforts to improve the quality of my play. Imagine how you would feel if the very same players you had defended with your blood and sweat on the ice, game after game, made you an object of their scorn." See, Shultz, *The Hammer*, 145.

and considered to be one of the NHL's best fighters, Shultz also lead the NHL in penalty minutes in the 1972-1973 season and in the 1973-1974 season.[179] Given the limited responsibilities of an enforcer, more often than not, they were exiled to their team's last line, and only called on by a coach when special circumstances arose, and their unique services needed. For former hockey enforcer Dwight Schofield, this simply meant they were largely "slaves" obligated to do the dirty work, situating some of them at the very bottom of the hockey player hierarchy.[180] Faced with precarious and often dangerous employment, having little or no education or employment skills to fall back on, and situated in a culture that physically exploited their bodies, the hockey enforcer was in many ways a working class man doing a working-class job.

Working Class Men

"Whatever his style on the ice, the [enforcer] remains a working man trying to do his job."[181]

- Gary Ronberg, *The Violent Game*, 1975

Men who became enforcers in the 1970s were made enforcers by their class position, much more than by their natures. It was largely working-class boys desiring to escape their limited economic opportunities who became hockey players in general and enforcers in particular. It was true that rich kids did not view the rough-and-tumble life of a hockey player in general, an enforcer in particular, as worth pursuing; too dangerous, far too precarious. Gary Ronberg, in his 1975 book *The Violent Game: A Close Look at Pro Hockey and its Bad Guys* argued that:

---

179 Although Schultz received fame and notoriety for his on ice actions, his own feelings toward his hockey antics was mixed: Here is Shultz explaining, "of course my inner feelings were not especially satisfying in terms of what I was doing. I had crossed the border from clean hockey to goon hockey and I can't say that I was inwardly happy about my destructive style. At times I felt embarrassed about my tantrums on the ice and at other times I felt a sense of shame over what I was doing to the game and its image." See, Shultz, *The Hammer*, 54.
180 Fischler, *Bad Boys*, 88-89.
181 Gary Ronberg, *The Violent Game: A Close Look at Pro Hockey and Its Bad Guys* (Englewood Cliffs, NJ: Prentice Hall, 1975), 166.

[F]rom its formative years, hockey has born the indelible stamp of the hard-working, hard-living, Canadian men who faced the hardships of the frontier with pride in their ability to endure punishment ... few players who had made it to the big league were well off when they were children. The rich kids usually gave up the earnest pursuit of hockey as too difficult, too demanding, and too dangerous. For those who made it to the big league, the game has traditionally been an escape from a life in the copper mine, a logging camp, or paper mill. A few broken bones or missing teeth were small price to pay.[182]

Ross Bernstein, author of *The Code: The Unwritten Rules of Fighting and Retaliation in the NHL* interviewed over 100 college hockey players and found how social class played a significant role in determining who became a professional hockey enforcer:

I [Bernstein] asked them [college players] why aren't more college guys making the jump to professional [hockey]. And resoundingly, they said there's such a leap from college to pro. They basically said each of these guys is going to have to take a few years, to go cut their teeth in the minor leagues and pay their dues. And they said, a lot of these guys realize that they might not be that great, and they're going to need to drop the gloves. And when you got a college degree to fall back on, you're not as tough as the kid from Moncton or Moose Jaw that realizes 'You know what, I have to make it. I've got nothing to fall back on other then a job in a salt mine' ... That is a huge factor of why a lot of these kids will do whatever it takes.[183]

Why, then, would a rich boy fight? Born to privilege, they didn't. In the same way rich boys did not fight in wars, or in the same way rich boys did not become professional boxers, rich boys did not become hockey

---

182 Ronberg, *The Violent Game*, 53.
183 David M. Singer, "Behind the Code: Interview with Ross Bernstein," January 15, 2007, http://www.hockeyfights.com

enforcers. Working class boys fought in wars; working class boys became professional boxers; and working class boys became hockey enforcers.[184]

But why would working class boys willingly become a hockey enforcer? Like boxers, working class boys realized early in life that it was primarily their fists and their capacity to inflict and endure pain that could be used to lift themselves out of a traditional working class life, into the life of a professional athlete. Consider the early life choices faced by well-known hockey enforcer Dave Schultz. Shultz had this to say in his 1980 autobiography, *Confessions of a Hockey Enforcer*, about the choices he faced as a working-class boy:

> [B]y the time I reached my mid teens there were only two real choices for me, farm work or hockey. In that sense I was like thousands of Canadian prairie kids before me. They instinctively turned away from the farm and toward the rink.After all, it was better to play with a hockey stick then a shovel.[185]

Like many of the enforcers that played during the 1970s, Dave Schultz came from a small rural town and had a childhood marked by poverty. In fact, the childhood circumstances that led Schultz to literally fight

---

184 Sometime ago, Bobby Neal, a former boxer and manager, who was nearly killed in the boxing ring defended boxing as a sport, despite the high levels of brutal violence. For Neal, most boxers box because, as working class boys, it is their only "escape from hard labor" or unemployment. See, Colin Radford, "Utilitarianism and the Noble Art," *Philosophy* 63 (1988), 70. Reflecting a similar thought, in *On Boxing*, Joyce Carol Oates writes that, "if boxers as a class are angry one would have to be willfully naïve not to know why. For the most part they constitute the disenfranchised of our affluent society, they are the sons of impoverished ghetto neighborhoods in which anger, if not fury, is appropriate." See, Joyce Carol Oates, *On Boxing* (New York, NY: Harbor Perennial, 2006), 63. When speaking about the relationship between poverty and boxers, legendary writer A. J. Liebling once wrote, "the [Great] depression killed the gate but it developed fighters." Writing in the 1950s he also mentions the way race and class came together as systems of oppression to produce boxers. Here is Liebling in 1952, quoting a boxing expert, "The only ones who work hard are the colored boys . . . because for them it's still tough outside. The good white fighters you got coming up, you could count them on your fingers." See, A. J. Liebling, *A Neutral Corner: Boxing Essays* (New York, NY: Farrar, Straus and Giroux, 1990), 5. Keep in mind, Canada's most famous boxer, George Chuvalo, a son of immigrant parents, grew up poor in Toronto in the 1950s. See, George Chuvalo with Murray Greig, *Chuvalo: A Fighter's Life* (Toronto, ON: HarperCollins, 2013). Discussing men's life chances in the American context, Christian G. Appy has documented the way in which social class determined which men fought in the Vietnam War. According to Appy, Vietnam, more than any other American war in the 20th century, perhaps in its history, "was a working-class war . . . roughly 80 percent of soldiers came from working-class and poor backgrounds." See, Christian G. Appy, *Working-Class War: American Combat Soldiers & Vietnam* (Chapel Hill, NC: The University of North Carolina Press, 1993).
185 Shultz, *The Hammer*, 29.

his way into the NHL were very similar to another well-known 1970s enforcer, Bob Plager.[186]

Bob Plager was born in 1943 and grew up in Kirkland Lake, Ontario. Kirkland Lake was a small working class community known for its coalmines. Plager's mother worked in the Kirkland Lake cafeteria, while his father, like so many working class men in the town worked the mines: "my dad and relatives all worked in the mines," Plager recalled. However, it wasn't only the men who worked the mines, children also went to labour down deep in the earth. Plager started mining at age 12. And, it was at the age of 12 when working down in the mines Plager was crushed by two coal cars. The accident forced him to spend the next two years in and out of hospitals. His horrific experience working in the mines was what fuelled Plager's hunger to pursue hockey as a career: "I [worked in the mines] as a kid, and it was so dark down there that all I could think was, 'Please God, get me out here. Let me see what the world is all about.' Hockey was my only way out. So I took it."[187] For white working class boys growing up in working class communities across Ontario, they often had two choices when they were growing up: "go into professional hockey or go into the mines."[188]

Or, take former Philadelphia Flyer Bobby Clarke. Clarke was not strictly what we would today associate with being an enforcer; he did have however have a strong reputation as a physical player, an agitator. Clarke was born in Flin-Flon, a mining town of about 2500 people, located on the border of Manitoba and Saskatchewan. As an industrial mining town, it was a place young men dreamt of leaving, a town on the way to everywhere but seldom a destination in itself. According to a February 23, 1976 *Sports Illustrated* cover story written by sports writer Ray Kennedy and featuring Bobby Clarke, "most of the 12,000 inhabitants worked for the Hudson Bay Mining and Smelting Company."[189] The men

---

186 Bob, Barclay and Bill Plager all played in the NHL and all were considered tough. Out of the three brothers, however, Bob was largely considered to have the strongest claim to being an enforcer. It is worth noting as well, that Barclay, or 'Barc the Spark' was also known as a very fierce competitor, accumulating over 1000 penalty minutes in 614 NHL games. The St. Louis Blues retired his number 8 in 1981, and he died on February 6, 1988 of a brain hemorrhage.
187 Ronberg, *The Violent Game*, 142.
188 Stan Fischler, *Gary Unger and the Battling Blues* (New York, NY: Dodd, Mead & Company, 1976), 126.
189 Ray Kennedy, "Dr. Jekyll and Mr. Clarke," Sports Illustrated, February 23, 1976, 58-71.

in the Clarke family were no exception. As a child, Clarke watched his father work down in the mines as a drilling inspector. The experience of watching his father spend his working life down in the mines motivated Clarke to pursue a hockey career. In fact, Clarke was very clear on the economic options available to him as a working class boy: "In Flin Flon you either play hockey or you work in the mines."[190] And for Clarke, "there's no way I wanted to work in those mines." For Clarke, like other working class boys, hockey provided him with life chances he would not ordinarily have been given. Let's take one more example, Dave Williams.

Dave Williams was born in 1954 and grew up in a working class, immigrant community in the small prairie town of Weyburn, Saskatchewan. According to his 1984 autobiography *Tiger: A Hockey Story*, Williams' grew up in the "poorest section of Weyburn" where his family did not own a car, a telephone or a television set. His father, the lone breadwinner of the family was a painter at the local "mental hospital." He earned "very little money." Williams recounted for readers how the material deprivations that he and his family faced during his childhood and how these material deprivations shaped his boyhood experiences:

> There are so many things that nagged at me. Not having a car for so many years, nor a telephone, put you at the mercy of other kids when it came to hockey. If I didn't get a lift or the use of the telephone I was finished. To get a message about changes in practice times or about special games, such as an all-star or Representative game, I had to leave the telephone number of the grocery store or neighbour's house and then check with them at a certain time. It took a lot of planning and you can wear yourself out collecting messages.[191]

There was more. Williams was also bothered as a child by the fact that his mother had to do the ironing after bringing the laundry in from the

---

190 Ibid.
191 Dave Williams with James Lawton. *Tiger: A Hockey Story* (Toronto, ON: Douglas & McIntyre, 1984), 32.

outside, where he mentioned it was often 30 below zero. Unlike many middle class homes, the Williams' family did not own a dryer for their wet clothes.

When it came to finding equipment to play hockey as a boy, Williams could not rely on his family's limited resources. Instead, he had to scrounge around for used skates, equipment and hockey sticks. For instance, Williams' described how he used to go the local arena to find hockey sticks that had been discarded by other players because they were broken. He told readers that he would use "special nails" from the hospital workshop where his father worked, along with glue and some tape in order to put the sticks back together. It was Williams' early experience growing up in a working class house where material wants and needs were not met, that played a significant role in shaping his desire to play hockey. It was, to put another way, his desire to heal the wounds inflicted by material deprivation that fuelled his desire to succeed in hockey. Tiger explained:

> My nickname came from the way I played hockey, but what I was most tigerish about, deep down, was the need to earn some money. It hurt that my dad didn't have a car. It hurt like hell, and it was a wound that never really healed . . . when I was starting out in hockey, one of the things that kept me going was the idea of that new car [for his dad] in the future. A lot of that really early hockey was filled with stops and starts, and that was hard for someone like me, a labourer on skates.[192]

Clearly, Tiger never forgot the conditions that came with living in poverty. His ongoing efforts to "heal" the raw "wound" caused by class conflict fuelled his desire to succeed in hockey.

Yet, equally important to the success of his career was his father's emphasis on teaching his sons to be appropriately masculine, including teaching Tiger and his brothers' how to fight. Coming close to articulating the infamous social Darwinist position, in that he implicitly suggested only the strong survive, his father conveyed to him that "if you

---

192 Williams, *Tiger*, 33.

were weak you had no chance at all" in life.[193] There was some truth to this, of course. In order to survive the hardscrabble life of working-class environments that are often marked by a traditional masculine ideology, one had to be tough and exhibit the capacity to stand up physically and otherwise to others, if need be. In Tiger's world growing up, he understood that a man's worth was largely dependent on his physical toughness. Once a man has demonstrated physical or emotional weakness, he was thought to become fair game for anyone and everyone to intimidate and take advantage of. For men or boys, physical or emotional weakness would often lead to marginalization and exclusion, as it is closely linked to a traditional femininity; which is to say, physical and emotional toughness are key characteristics that was thought to clearly separate the sexes.

So with this as a guiding principle, Tiger pursued success on the hockey rink with a physical toughness that many other players simply could not match. And, without a doubt, male hockey players such as Tiger were very much aware that their moral identity in the eyes of other men was primarily secured by being undeniably tough. Chicago Blackhawk's enforcer Keith Magnuson understood clearly the relationship between physical toughness and moral worth in the context of professional hockey: "Here is [o]ne thing you got to have to be a success in this league can't be taught ... the ingredient is guts-and this means not being afraid of anyone," Magnuson exclaimed.[194] For Magnuson, his capacity to be tough was all meant to demonstrate a level of control over an opponent, a clear sense of physical and emotional dominance, which in the context of traditional masculine hierarchies brought with it a high level of masculine respect. The player who allowed others to control his game in such an obvious way came to be viewed as weak, or less than a man. All of which led to the conclusion that the team that wins has the most 'masculine' men, or so the argument ran.

In the 1970s, within the world of boys and men, humiliation meant emasculation. Humiliate a boy or man and you took away his masculinity. For male hockey players in the 1970s, humiliation had to be avenged,

---

193 Ibid., 31.
194 Doug Feldman, *Keith Magnuson: The Inspiring Life and Times of a Beloved Blackhawk* (Chicago, IL: Triumph Books, 2013), 179.

or, you ceased to be a man. Aggrieved entitlement is a gendered emotion, then, a fusion of that humiliating loss of masculinity and the moral and ethical obligation and entitlement to get back. Humiliation was so injurious to men's psyche, so threatening to the identity of themselves as 'real men' and as 'real hockey players' it had to be healed. It was this fear of being humiliated or embarrassed in front of teammates and other men, coaches, and fans, that male hockey players feared most. As 1970s pro-hockey player Derek Sanderson recently explained in his 2012 autobiography:

> I started playing hockey when I was eight, and that was one of thefirst things my dad had me thinking about: conditioning myself to ignore pain and never allowing it to intimidate me. And it never did. Getting beat up? That didn't bother me. Cut, bleeding, broken bones? That didn't bother me. Fear of embarrassment and fear of rejection – that bothered me. Losing a fight in front of allthose people, whether it was in junior or the NHL, was my greatest fear in hockey.[195]

The fear of humiliation, appearing weak and less masculine in front of others, of being dominated by another man, pushed men into action that sometimes bordered on criminal behaviour. Dave Forbes, a retired Boston Bruins hockey player was tried in a criminal court in the summer of 1975 for aggravated assault after butt-ending Henry Boucha's eye socket in a game against the Minnesota North Stars. The trial received much attention, as it was highly unusual at that time for an athlete to face criminal charges for actions taken in the course of competition. The trial ended with the jury unable to reach a decision and the charges dropped. Yet, the incident clearly had an impact on Forbes:

> What would make me do such a thing? I don't have an answer for that. I do know I was a little punchy, a little lost that night.

---

195 Derek Sanderson with Kevin Shea, *Crossing The Line: The Outrageous Story of a Hockey Original* (Toronto, ON: HarperCollins, 2012), 16.

Then, when Boucha punched me early in the first, I remember thinking, 'What's this? Things aren't bad enough but now I have to catch it from this guy?' I was probably a little embarrassed, humiliated. I'd been put down, made to look like a fool, and I felt that I had to prove myself so that coach would think better of me. So I kept pumping myself. I could feel my stomach going … and then it happened.[196]

Forbes' testimony clearly reveals the way in which humiliation of one man by another man became a key factor in violent confrontations, especially in the context of hyper masculine sports such as hockey.

Hockey enforcers rarely succeeded in school. They simply did not view it as a legitimate choice. Dave Williams, for example, told readers that he learned at a young age that "if I was going to get anywhere in the world, it wasn't going to be through a schoolbook."[197] Tiger, of course, was not alone in his rejection of school. At a relatively young age, David Schultz also rejected school, viewing his schooling experience as a waste of time. Their views are not surprising as working-class boys in general were often encouraged to be tough, athletic, and super macho, not smart or academically successful. Boys who were academically successful at school were thought to be wimps or sissies. Instead, working-class boys were pushed to play sport, encouraged to fight, and to disdain school work as academic success in school has been historically associated with traditional femininity. Working class boys were not encouraged to be responsible in a traditional sense or be "goody-goody." To do so, would place them too close to an assumed traditional femininity. Rather, working class boy were taught to be wild, take risks, and compete physically, emotionally and psychologically with other men. The socialization of working-class boys functioned to prepare them for jobs in construction, policing or military, coal mining, the steel mills, the auto factories, or other forms of factory work. It also prepared them to work with their fists on the rink.

---

196 Ray Kennedy, "Wanted: An End to Mayhem," *Sports Illustrated*, November 17, 1975, 16-21.
197 Williams, Tiger, 39.

It was the relationship between the enforcer and work on which ideas of the respectability of the working-class rested. Work was central to the performance of more admired forms of white male working class identities. For white workingmen in the American context, paid employment has for sometime now signalled a form of moral decency. Simply put, to be considered an 'appropriate' man by other men, one had to work; a man was required to be the breadwinner. To be otherwise, unemployed for instance, positioned you as less than a man.[198] This of course, posed something of a problem to hockey enforcers. Like other working-class men, enforcers were faced with precarious employment. Lose a fight or two, and you would find yourself playing in the minors, or out of hockey altogether. And the math was simple- out of hockey, out of a job. For those who were given the role of enforcer, the choice was very simple: conform to the demands of the role or risk losing your job. Even during good times enforcers never felt completely secure because of the limited duration of their work. Enforcers were working-class boys who took working-class jobs, but became at least symbolically something much more in the context of the 1970s. Against the backdrop of significant social, political and economic change, hockey enforcers became working class heroes to the white working class and middle-class males who cheered them on. It is to this issue that I briefly turn my attention.

White Working Class Heroes

The hockey enforcer came to hold a special appeal among many hockey fans, the general public, and the media. Throughout the 1970s, hockey enforcers were promoted and popularized not only on the basis of whiteness but also on the basis of their perceived working-class nature, at a time when white working-class identities were in the words of then pres-

---

198 Male unemployment is one of the key challenges to a man's masculinity. Being fully committed to the breadwinner ideology carries real consequences for men's health. For instance, the president of the Anxiety Disorders Association of Ontario reported that traditionally men made up only about 30% of their clients, whereas, following the economic downturn in 2009 the number jumped to almost 50%. The Mental Health Commission of Canada reported that men were calling crises lines and joining support groups in unprecedented numbers once the recession hit. See, C. J. Greig and Susan Holloway, "Canadian Manhood(s)," in *Canadian Men and Masculinities: Historical and Contemporary Perspectives*, edited by Christopher J. Greig and Wayne Martino (Toronto, ON: Canadian Scholars' Press, 2013), 119-138.

ident Richard Nixon in 1969, "forgotten." Set against the backdrop of the Vietnam War, Watergate and the Cold War, and limited by economic recession, hit with the emerging energy crisis, inflation, stagflation, globalization, deregulation, and faced with large-scale social and political change brought on by the civil rights movement and second wave feminism and its embrace of new racial, gender and cultural priorities, white working and middle class males began to feel, not only aggrieved, alienated, but 'forgotten.' Increasingly bitter, cynical, anxious and resentful over the slow erosion of their privilege and sense of entitlement, white male hockey fans and others, came to view the rough and tumble, white male 'hockey enforcer' as a symbol of hope.

High profile enforcers from the 1970s such as Dave Shultz and John Wensink offered hockey fans and others a symbol of the 'forgotten man', a self-made man who embodied historically prized masculine values of strength, individualism, toughness, and determination, at that time when white working-class males were anxious and fearful that 'normalcy' was being undermined by large scale changes in society. To put differently, the white hockey hero-enforcer, whose masculinity confirmed the values of patriarchy, the work ethic and rugged individualism, and who clearly demarcated the boundaries between men and women, black and white, heterosexual and homosexual became, if nothing more, a symbol, an expression, and an outlet for white male middle and working class anxieties and frustrations in the age of retrenchment.

Take, for example, the testimony of Boston Bruin fan, Tom Gleason, who recently commented on 1970s Boston Bruin enforcer, John Wensink. Gleason's comments, however, need to be understood in the context of the desegregation of Boston public schools. In response to the passing of the 1965 Racial Imbalance Act, which ordered Boston public schools in Massachusetts to desegregate as a way to address racial inequality, a plan was laid out for compulsory busing of students between predominantly white and black areas of the city. The forced busing of black students into predominately white areas, and white students into predominately black areas caused significant unrest, causing a number of violent protests. At this time Boston was literally a tinderbox, filled with significant racial and class-based tensions, ready to explode.

Gleason recalled the night of December 1, 1977, in the Boston Garden. The Bruins were playing the expansion Minnesota North Stars. During the game, Bruin enforcer John Wensink fought Minnesota North Star player Alex Pirus. After pummeling Pirus, Wensink skated immediately to challenge the entire Minnesota North Star bench to a fight. Famously, no North Star player took Wensink up on his challenge. Filmed for ESPN's sport based documentary series '30-30 Shorts' and titled "Our Tough Guy," here is Gleason remembering the incident and, more importantly the social and political context in which it took place:

> You have to remember that back in 1977, Boston had just gone through busing. The people wanted to send their children to their own neighborhood schools, and they weren't allowed that anymore. So, the city was tense, uptight, and we sort of lived through our Bruins. That night when the fights broke out, Boston fans loved it, because it gave them something to cheer about . . . You are not going to mess with the Bruins, you are not going to mess with John Wensink, and you're not going to mess with this city.[199]

As the quote above suggests, Wensink became much more than simply a hockey enforcer, but became a momentary symbol of resistance for white working and middle class men in the face of social, political, and economic change. And, of course, Wensink is probably best understood by readers as a pawn himself; a flashpoint for larger, much more complex and much more troubling set of social, political and economic problems.

By the 1970s in urban industrial places like Boston and Philadelphia the 'law and order' that the lower-middle class white men had based their life on was now thought threatened by a range of significant social, political, economic changes. 'Traditional' values such as hard work, order, authority, competitive struggle, and self-reliance that had not only underwritten the 'American Dream', but came to define the existence of working and middle class white males, were now thought to be un-

---

199 ESPN 30-30 Shorts, "Our Tough Guy," directed by Molly Schiot (2014).

dermined by changes brought on by the civil rights movement and second wave feminism and other forms of social and political upheaval. Of course, the idea of 'traditional' values was neatly conflated with a white working class hetero-masculinity, and as a consequence those who did not fit into this particular identity-women, blacks, sexual minorities, the poor and 'others'-were accused of undermining the so-called traditional values when they began to agitate for change.

Throughout the 1970s, the so-called forgotten-man was presented to the public as speaking for and the embodiment of 'traditional' values. In this sense, traditional values, which are best understood as – patriarchal, class-based, racist and hetero-normative – were linked with white masculinity that escaped the perceived 'softness' thought to be pervading American culture in the wake of the 'permissive' 1960s. For white working class males during the 1970s, it was an anxious time as they feared that 'normalcy' was being eroded by significant changes in society, the group of others were threatening to invalidate the very terms of the very category that the forgotten-man would seem to depend. The increasing presence of gays, lesbians and bisexuals in society, ran along side concerns over the breakdown of the nuclear family and the rise of female led households, did little to comfort those wedded to traditional notions of 'normalcy.' The forgotten-man became increasingly perceived within popular and professional discourse as wounded, weakened and vulnerable.

Of course, this particular discourse did very little to undermine in any significant way the power and position of white masculinity, but it did enable white men to make equity rights claims and ask for compensation or restitution for their alleged injuries. The notion that emerged in the late 60s and into the 1970s was that white men were now an object of discrimination; a moment when white masculinity started to assert equity claims based on group rights and wrongs, while at the same time holding onto the privilege and power that comes precisely with their membership in this particular group. The overriding tension that existed between white men's equity claims and the privilege and power that they as a group possessed was at the heart of the rise in popularity of the hockey enforcer.

A key feature of this particular discourse during the 1970s, however, was the idea that white males lost what was 'rightfully' assumed to be theirs including well paid jobs; they experienced a deep alienation from the social system that by rights, they dominated. The perceived 'special treatment' afforded non-white minorities and women through various policy initiatives allowed mostly white working and middle-class males to complain that no one was speaking for them. In a chapter titled, "Working-Class Youth: Alienation Without an Image," published in the 1970 edited collection, *The White Majority*, two sociologists put it this way "He feels powerless and often feels himself to be the object manipulation, someone who is exploited or poorly served by the central institutions of his society. He feels that other groups in the society– both above and below him– are getting more than their share and getting it by not playing by the rules, particularly the rule that says you have to pay for what you get."[200] Simon and Gagnon go on to write, "if he is not isolated, he feels an increasing sense of cultural desertion–the society may be involved into many things he cannot experience or get to. He has values that he shares with his friends and family, but not necessarily with the larger society."[201] Part of that lost entitlement was the power to represent the idea of America and to determine the conditions and terms of so called American normativity, largely based on white, male, middle-class and Protestant values. It was in this sense that privilege and power of whiteness was threatened. White males became agitated at a set of others' (mostly women and non-whites) use of the logic victimization, so they simply positioned themselves as victims. No longer able to understand a world in which they had grown accustomed to, social commentators and others routinely argued that white men felt invisible, forgotten, discontented and resentful. The rise and popular fascination with the hockey enforcer during the decade of the 1970s, then, would never have been possible had it not tapped into a rich vein of white lower and middle class male discontentment and growing anger at broader social and political change.

In fact, change itself became the problem. Some of the racism and

---

200 William Simon and John B. Gagnon, "Working Class Youth: Alienation Without Image," in *The White Majority: Between Poverty and Affluence*, edited by Louise Kapp Howe (New York, NY: Vintage Books, 1970), 58.
201 Ibid.

sexism being challenged by the civil rights movement and second wave feminism came to represent for white working-class males the most powerful symbols of disruptive change in their lives. These symbols were perceived by white working-class men as being endorsed or at least tolerated by the major institutions of society such as schools, the government and the legal system. It was this endorsement or perhaps even promotion by various institutions that generated a certain kind of white rage. Thus, white working-class men also became anti-establishment, but for them it was the so-called perceived liberal establishment they came to resent, and before it they felt increasingly alienated and powerless. Adding to his frustration was the fact that he could not take the alternative of "dropping out." For white working class men, there was no place to drop out to. He did not seek out change; it sought him, so the argument ran. It was these social, political and economic changes that created the demand among white working-class males for something akin to 'a great white hope,' a man who would at least symbolically defeat those groups who were agitating for social and political change. To some degree, the white hockey enforcer, then, came to symbolize a man fighting against society, a society that was increasingly being perceived as discriminating against white working-class men.

Conclusion

The rise of the hockey enforcer was primarily due to a number of complex and overlapping historical factors. The NHL expansion in 1967 and the emergence of the rival 'Rebel' league (WHA), created a much-expanded demand for the labour of hockey players. An outcome of this new demand was the fact that players who were less skilled but more able to be physically violent made their way onto professional hockey teams. Professional teams actively sought out one or two players whose sole role would be to fight opponents and intimidate other teams. It was also clear that the men who would become professional enforcers in the 1970s largely came from working-class backgrounds. Rejecting the school system's invitation to learn, hockey became one of the only ways in which they could escape their economic and material conditions. Yet, while certainly being a professional hockey player brought them monetary wealth and social status, the job itself was working-class in nature. Rooted in physical and emotional violence and subject to precarious employment, the job itself put the men at physical risk. The hockey enforcers of the 1970s were working-class men doing a working-class job.

At a deeper level, in the mid to late 1970s hockey enforcers became a symbol of hope to other white men in the context of large-scale social, political and economic changes. To be sure, the 1970s was also a time of diminished expectations for white men, in particular middle and working-class men. In contrast, the 1950s and 1960s were clearly time periods where white male heterosexual privilege was simply taken for granted, and simply unquestioned. Due to economic, political and social change, the 1970s marked the beginning, to some measure, of the erosion of white-middle and working class male privilege and power, all of which gave rise to the popularity of the hockey enforcer.

CHAPTER FIVE:
Ice: A Micro Hockey Ethnography

R aising and educating premier athletes in a nation's sport is never easy. It takes an overwhelming commitment and investment of
personal time, money, and social networking to develop hockey players
in Canada. This chapter allows the reader to step inside the composite
rink life of one goalie, one player, and a mother—with sideline commen-
tary from several National Hockey League (NHL) experts, during the
Spring tryouts for their elite teams in Canada. Explore the personalities
found next to the ice. Experience the thoughts and personas of players
and their parents, and explore the intimate web of elite hockey culture,
motivations for playing and a hockey life-in-narrative typically found in
small-town Canadian communities.

Goalie Ice

We were strangers. We moved into a new house to begin new careers and
jobs, a 'new hockey boundary' for our sons. They loved their old teams,
the players, and the coaches, especially my youngest son Jake, an AAA
goalie. Jake had played with relatively the same group of boys for three
years, and had led his team to two divisional championships in those
years. The boys were close, had fun on and off the ice, and the coaches,
fathers of players on the team, were an organized, genuinely nice group

of dads.

What we loved about the team is that, generally, we were a small community that knew everyone, so we felt at home in that arena. The larger center we were in was new: we didn't know any of the parents, none of the coaches, Jake didn't know any of the other players (except the odd one that seemed familiar from a tournament or two).

Although we were leaving our old 'hockey family' behind, we thought it would be a positive experience for Jake to play with new people and to perhaps learn different skills in a new league. There is also an advantage to not knowing anyone in a new centre: you don't have any pre-conceived notions or opinions about anyone. As an outsider, everyone you meet is a positive, warm individual with only the best interests of the team at heart. (Most people would not think this naivety is good when walking into the political web of tryout season.)

Tryout season in hockey comes at the end of a long and winding nine-month road of daily practices and weekend games and tournaments leading up to a scoreboard of provincial rankings. And never during the year are the behind-the-scene politics more intense than in May. In smaller centres, where 'everyone knows everyone,' people say that the 'team is already picked before they get on the ice.' And maybe this is true. Certainly in the later years, for e.g., PeeWee or Bantam, the rosters don't fluctuate a whole lot unless someone moves. I know moving Jake opened up a spot for an AA goalie who had been wanting to play AAA for two or three years, so it was wonderful for that new team.

Before tryouts begin, there are 'tryouts' for the coaches. Hockey associations interview interested coaches a month before the posted OMHA tryout dates. Parents will write letters of support, or against, coaches they like, or don't like, and usually such appointments come with some 'unwritten understandings.' In our area, most coaches have sons that play at the same level, and those children make the team. That is 'understood'. I've never really had a problem with it. If a parent is going to be gone from home three to four nights a week, and on weekends, volunteering all that time to others, then why shouldn't their child benefit from it? (How much ice time they get as a result, well, that is always widely discussed in the stands).

Another common understanding for those coaches selected is that the parents who assist as trainers or managers will have children on the team as well. In the centre we moved into, the manager on the team had a son who had played goalie the year prior and was trying out again. This was a red flag to us that there was only one goalie position open for Jake's year, since teams only take two goalies, and they weren't likely to be cutting the manager's boy.

Since we didn't know anyone on the team, or in the area, we emailed the association first to let them know that we would be attending tryouts that May. The woman who telephoned me back told me, "They haven't chosen a coach yet for your son's year because two of the parents from last year had a big fight with the coach, yelling matches back and forth in the changerooms, then suspensions from the arena, so they're looking for a new coach. Should I put you on the email list?" "Ah, sure," I said.

That didn't give me a harmonious first impression, but then I am sure the new coach would spend time mending and bonding.

We never did get an email from the association, and nothing ever went up on the website, so when I called back, the woman said, "the first try-out is tonight. 5 p.m."

That was in an hour! I had to leave work early, pick up Jake at the school and his equipment, and we hurried to the first tryout at a strange arena with twenty minutes to change.

Jake was nervous on the way. He's usually a chatterbox, but tonight he was silently, grey, staring straight ahead. For a goalie, so much of the game is mental. You are by yourself in practice, you are on your own in a game. I think that's why Patrick Roy named his stick "Charlotte" and talked to his posts, "Hey guys, if I don't get it, you get it okay?"[202] He was lonely. His coach Allaire called it "visualization," but I believe Roy just wanted to feel as if he had some people with him at the net.

We parked, and before we left the car, I said to Jake, "Who are you?"

"I'm a guardian of the net," he said.

"What are you?" I said.

"I'm strong, smart speed," he said.

"Okay, then just go do what you love to do," I said and kissed him.

That was our routine before every game. Goalies need to focus, med-itate, get 'into the zone'. Players, on the other hand, need to pump-up

---

202 Michel Roy, Patrick Roy: *Winning. Nothing Else* (Mississauga, ON: John Wiley & Sons Canada, Ltd., 2007), 56.

into near-bursting energy.

Because there wasn't much time to change, I asked the woman at the sign-in desk which number changeroom they were in, then told Jake to just go ahead and change while I filled out the forms and paid the fees.

In this Centre, it cost $100 to try out for the team. $100 guaranteed Jake three 'skate-outs', then he could be cut, or "released", at which point he would have to pay another $100 to try out for the AA hockey team, and again on down the line until he made a team.

I got a frosty reception from the woman who was signing players in. She happily chatted away to the mother in front of me, they had probably known each other for awhile, then when I smiled and introduced myself, she said, "oh, so you're the people from out of town."

"Yes, we're new, just moved here. My son Jake is a goalie and is excited about the tryouts," I beamed my warmest smile.

"Fill these out. That's $100," she said flatly.

"Thank you so much," I said, then filled out the usual liability form *("If he dies and it's your responsibility I still won't sue...")* and commitment sheets for her as quickly as possible.

What I later found out was that the registrar's best friend's son was also trying out for goalie, so I really didn't have a chance with her.

Paul Valliant of British Columbia writes that, "parents must realize they need to interact congenially with others; they must learn to fabricate positive relationships which support their child's involvement in the sport."[203]

And I believe that's true. When we arrived at the arena that day, the first thing I found out was that the 'second goalie' (not the manager's son) was cut the year before because the mother fit into almost every one of Michel Roy's 'negative species of parents' list. She was so aggravating that no coach wanted the goalie on their team any longer, and the goalie had been relegated to the house leagues because of the parent's behaviour.

Valliant advises parents to "fabricate positive relationships;"[204] that is, they don't have to be real, but you can at least give the appearance of

---

203 Paul M. Valliant, *Minor Hockey to NHL: Parents survival guide* (Victoria, BC: Trafford Publishing, 2007), 28.

204 Ibid.

good etiquette.

I have been around arena politics a long time, and if I am staying to watch a game or a practice (sometimes I just drop off because I have a job and other children), then I have three core principles that guide my behavior:

> 1. Never, ever, ever *EVER* get drawn into saying anything bad or defamatory about another player or parent. Gossips will try to draw you into conversations about ice time (too much; not enough), lines, this player hogging the puck, that player doing this-or-that, but don't respond. Just smile and nod, and ask if you can get them a coffee, then don't come back. Or if you do, change the subject.

> 2. Don't talk hockey. Talk about work, or funny stories about school, or home, or husbands, or the NHL, but don't talk about the hockey team.

> 3. Give one specific compliment to one person each time you're in the arena, and

> 4. On the way home, be positive. No matter how unbelievably bad the game was, never, ever, ever *EVER* say anything negative. Especially about other players. It will be circulating snapchat and the changerooms before you know it.

I was nervous for Jake in this new arena, so I went to sit down next to the ice. I didn't know any of the other women, so I sat by myself at the end of one side across from the goal where Jake had been sent. In arenas, the men tend to watch by the windows or glass, and most of the women tend to either sit inside or in the stands in small groups. It's like a dinner party—the women stand and chat in one area, while the men mingle in another.

There were six goalies on the ice, but only one position up for grabs. The goalies alternated in goal between every fifth player, or shot, then they would wait in line until it was their turn to go in again. That's pretty common. Jake had a psychological advantage with the coaches though. There's a mystique in hockey that 'all the best players' evolve from country ice ponds, sharpening their skates and skills in the great outdoors, until someone puts them on a tiny indoor rink in Toronto to shine. I am not quite sure where this myth comes from, but there's not a hockey book today that doesn't support this idea. We were from one of those 'back country ice areas', so the coaches viewed Jake as if he were some untapped diamond. In fact, Jake had played indoor rep[resentative] hockey for most of his years skating, so he didn't know a pond from Adam, but if the brand helped him, who am I to dispel it?

I sat in the stand that first tryout hoping that Jake would get noticed. I prayed that the posts would help block shots, that he looked confident. When the gates opened for the ice to be flooded, I went out into the hallway to wait for Jake to change. I was standing beside a mother with a bright purple streak through her hair.

"Do you have someone trying out?" she said.

"Yes, a goalie, Jake, in the blue jersey," I smiled.

"Oh, I saw him, he looked great," she said, "I'm Jenn, Brendan's mother, #45."

"Oh, the fast one!" I said.

She looked pleased and we talked about when the next practice was and when the coach would likely make the first round of cuts.

I made a friend! I thought.

Jake came out smiling and wet. I smiled at Jenn, and said, "Okay, see you Thursday!"

We'll see.

Tryout #1 Tally of Cost:

$100 Registration
+ $12.50 in Gas
+ $5.72 at Tim's

Total: $118.22

Needing an Edge and One Less Goal

Moving houses and centres, a rushed beginning, and not knowing any-one is enough to throw any athlete off of his game, and this is how Jake felt after week one of tryouts. I picked Jake up outside of the arena on Friday night. He threw his equipment into the car, then slumped down into the passenger seat.

"You get cut?" Jake's brother asked.

"No, not yet, but I played like crap," he replied.

"When do you find out? Did they say anything?" I asked.

This was the end of the first three tryouts, and major cuts were going to be made before the next practice. Jake said that the coach was going to put the names of those invited back online, and that one or two play-ers would be "signed" before the next tryout.

Every centre is different. Some coaches like to speak to each player individually, assess their skills and what they need to work on, then let them know if they've been "released" or "signed". They're funny terms for a bunch of 13-year-olds, employment terms. It's more gentle than "cut" I guess. "We 'release you' into the wild. Go! And be free!" Although being 'cut down' is closer to what it feels like for the player.

That night, Jake checked the internet every five minutes, Refresh, Re-fresh, Refresh.

"What if the guy doesn't post it till Monday?" his brother said, "You going to wait there all night?"

At 9:35am the results went up. There were 20 players invited back, including three goalies. Jake made the cut. The players who had been signed had a little * next to their names, and this included the team manager's son, one of the three goalies, so Jake would need to beat the other goalie out for a spot on the team.

We found out later that the next two tryouts were also away games in Peterborough and Mississauga, and that Jake would be splitting the ice time in net with the other unsigned goalie.

"What do you think they're looking for?" Jake asked his dad the next night at supper.

"A shutout dufus," his older brother said, "don't let any goals in!"

"Right." Jake moped.

There are basically two styles of goaltending: One, the 'plug the net' style where the largest body possible stays as close to the crease as possi-ble so that every bit of surface area is covered. 'Plugging the net' allows very few high and slap shots, but it also means that defenders have to work extra hard to clear the rebounds and back ice because the goalie doesn't come out to pass shots. Two, the 'come out and pass' style where a mobile goalie comes out of his net to play low shots, pass off dumps, or cut the angle on slap shots from the blue line. The disadvantage of coming out is that it leaves the net open for fast skaters and breakaways. Goalies just don't skate that well with all that equipment on.

Coaches usually prefer one style over the other, but we didn't really know this coach, so didn't know what his preference might be, and didn't really know who to ask. Jake was a 'plug-the-net' goalie. He rarely came out of his net or passed off. Not knowing anyone on the team, we called the coach to ask about the games, 'What should he wear?' 'How early should he be there?' 'What will you be looking for?'

This way, paired with the details of the 'place and time', the question regarding the coach's goalie assessment didn't seem so out of place.

"Just tell him not to let any goals in," the coach laughed.

"Well, I guess your brother was right," Jake's dad said to him after he got off of the phone, "you're going to have to keep the net as clean as possible, or, at least, let in fewer goals than the other goalie."

We wanted to help Jake prep as much as possible prior to the two games, so we recruited his brothers and a couple of their friends, and brought them all out to the local ice early one morning before school. Their job was to work on getting Jake out of his goal as far as possible. Jake knew this too. He knew he would have to feel confident coming out to play the puck if he was going to separate himself from the other goalie.

"Come-on Jakee, come get me," they teased, "come get the puck."

And it worked. Because there was just a group of friends, not a high-stakes game, Jake did come out every time. His passing was prepped for the Petes.

The night before his game, Jake's Uncle Brian called as well. He's a marathon runner, so Brian went through a series of positive visualization exercises over the phone with him just before Jake went to bed. Goalies usually need to go over the kinds of shooters and shots they're going to see the day before a game. It gives their minds time to store the scenarios in advance of having to perform them.

The day of the game, I was nervous, but Jake seemed relaxed and calm.

"Who are you?" I said to Jake

"I'm the guardian of the net," he said.

"What are you?" I said.

"I'm strong, smart speed," he said.

"Okay, then go do what you love to do," I said and kissed him.

He smiled and went in to change.

I recall asking Jake once, "What is it exactly that you like about playing net?"

"The danger," he replied. He liked the feeling of being on the edge and that at any moment something dangerous was going to happen to him.

"Ha! Well, I guess it's a good thing you're a goalie then!" I said.

It's difficult for a goalie's mom to watch a game. You are so nervous for them. It's different with the other boys. They're players; if the puck goes by them, there's still the goalie there to stop it. But if it goes by Jake … the team has just lost a point. Win a game, and everyone loves you, tackles you in joy. Lose a game, and you're the most hated person in the arena.

I remember watching an Olympic game once with Carey Price in net, and his mother and girlfriend were sitting way up in the corner of the arena in the stands. They could have had tickets anywhere they wanted, but it was just too nerve-racking. Each time there was a shot on net, Price's mother covered her eyes in fear. I don't think they enjoyed a moment of the Winter games.

When the game starts, I say a silent prayer that Jake's net will be sealed with an invisible wall. I pray that he will anticipate the shots—that he will see and connect with everything. He has a fairly clean first few minutes, then there is a scramble in front of the net, and the puck pops over the line. My stomach drops. I feel ill. But Jake just turns around and takes a drink of water, then composes himself for the next onslaught. Well, so much for a clean net.

By the time he leaves the ice half way through the second, he has let in two goals. "He didn't let them in," my husband says, "they scored on them." *'Whatever. Same thing,'* I think.

Some statisticians argue that a goalie's save percentage should be based upon the type of goal scored, not just any goal scored. For example, is it harder to save a scramble, a slap shot from the blue line, or a screened shot? They're all very different skills. But most coaches are not goalie specialists. They just want to know, 'did you keep the net clean or not?'

In the second half, I shamefully pray that the other goalie lets in three. I know that doesn't sound charitable, but I also know that it will come down to final numbers and I hope that Jake's half is cleaner. In the second, the rest of the players pick up their game, and most of the play is in the opposing end. There are very few shots on our net; which normally is good, unless you are trying out as a goalie. Two quick soft goals are scored later into the third period, so the two goalies hold relatively the same percentage. I say a silent, *'Thank you!'*

Just before the buzzer goes, a foul is called, and the Petes score on their power play. The game ends 3-5. The coach tells the players in the dressing room that he's going to be signing some players tonight, and that by the next game, the rest of the cuts will be made. We wait a long time after the game. Eventually, the coach comes out of the dressing rooms and says, "I haven't decided about the goalies yet; let's wait until after the next game."

By the next game, the entire team has been picked, except the second goalie, so it's down to Jake's performance in this game. After travelling two hours to get to the arena, we say, "Well, at least you'll know after the game today. Just go out there, and do what you love Jake!"

The next game has a slightly better result for Jake: he only let in one goal. "You mean, 'they scored' once," my husband corrects me.

'Whatever. Same thing,' I think again.

After the game, we wait for the coach to talk to Jake, but he is in a hurry to get back home and simply says, "Sorry, I'll let you know later tonight."

Jake just shrugs and says, "I'm staaaaarving, can we get Subway?"

"I suppose so," my husband laughs and Jake orders a 12" Italian cold cut with grated cheese to sink his teeth into on the way home.

Two days go by, we haven't heard anything, nothing has been posted on the internet, and Jake is frantic with wonder, *"When* will I know? Can you call him Mom?"

For players released early from an AAA club, they have time to try out for a second or third club in their area, if the dates coincide, but Jake has been in tryouts for three weeks now, so if he is cut, he won't have time to try out for another AAA team. A friend he made during the first tryout was cut on day three, and subsequently made the last tryout date for the neighbouring AAA club. If Jake is cut in this round, his next option is to tryout for the AA team in the area. Beginning at age 7, children can try out for 'select travel teams.' At this age, there are two levels in the sport: houseleague and travel. By age 8-9, depending on the size of the city you live in, those levels increase to three or four: houseleague, AE, AA and AAA. If the centre is large, like Toronto, Laval, or Vancouver, there may be two AA or AAA teams in one city. The higher your level, the more practice and ice time the team is allocated by the league, and as a result, the higher the cost of playing. For boys in Canada, playing on an AA or AAA team carries a lot of social status.

That evening, we call the coach to ask, "Do you know when they might let Jake know at all?"

"It's been a difficult decision because the other goalie has been with the club a long time," he says, "let me call you back."

"Okay," my husband shrugs and hangs up puzzled.

"What'd he say?" I ask.

"He says he'll call back."

A few minutes later, the coach calls back and says, "okay, we're going to sign Jake, but you can't say anything to him until tomorrow because we can't get ahold of the other parents just yet."

"Okay," my husband says, while Jake and I watch him.

He hangs up and shrugs again.

Just then, the telephone rings yet again.

"It's me," the coach says, "it's okay, you can tell him now. I just got ahold of the parents."

"Would you like to tell him?" my husband asks, and passes the phone to Jake.

"Hello?" Jake says when he takes the phone.

"Jake?" the coach says, "we're going to sign you with the Grizzlies. Is that all right?"

"Yeah!" says Jake, "thank you, sir!"

"Okay Jake, tell your parents we have a few forms to fill out, and report for training in August," says the coach.

"Okay," says Jake grinning.

"I made it!" says Jake when he gets off of the phone.

"Are you happy?" we ask.

"Yeah, of course, but what do I do for the next two months?"

Tryout Total Tally of Cost:

Registration
+ 625km
+ Subway/Tim's
+ Ice Rental

Total: $619.50

Player Ice

Tanner is use to the tryout season. At his senior age of 14, he has had six major tryouts for his local 'rep' team, and it has been the same basic cohort of boys trying out each year. When he walks into the arena on this sunny Spring day, parents call out to him, "Hey Tanner, how're you doing? Back for more punishment?" He grins, signs his name and his position ('LW', left wing), pays his $100 tryout fee, and the convenor behind the registration table hands him a jersey.

"Changerooms 2 or 4," the convenor says.

Players never wear their own numbers or jerseys on the ice. To make it as impartial as possible, most teams will assign random numbers to players, then non-parent coaches are asked to sit in the stands and note the numbers they like for: skating, checking, passing, puck handling, scoring, and general ability to be a 'team player.'

Tanner is a skater. He's there because he loves the speed. When asked why he loves the game so much, he always says:

I play hockey because it fuels me with power and life.

People outside of a world of hockey think that the reason for playing is winning, or goals, or even institutionalized violence-on-ice, but if you are a hockey player - if it is part of your raison d'être - then you know that winning is not the number one reason why you play.

One of the oldest coaches in our area, and one of the first players ever to get a university scholarship for playing, once told me that he didn't care if he won or lost as long as one thing happened on the ice: If he had one great pass - one connection with that elusive black puck from the end of his stick, all the way through the mathematical maze of players, to the end of his line partner's stick – bam. That one click on the ice made him happier than anything else that might happen that wholenight. It dynamically stimulated him to perform that pass again and again and again. That power of connecting on ice was like an addiction.

My addiction is not the one great pass, or the dangle, or the deke, or the goal. My drug is speed on steel. Jumping over the boards onto sleek, wet Zamboni ice, and feeling that cold arena

air rush by on the way into the corner; it breeds power. I enjoy the race, from one blue line past opponents into their end.
Beating defenders down their own ice to that sliding piece of
rubber. I love feeling my thighs burn. Skating until that second
wind of speed kicks you into overdrive to reach through the
pain past everyone in sight.

Puck speed. That's why I play.

There is an accepted culture in each arena across Canada during tryout
season. Fathers and grandfathers will cluster around the glass next to
the rink with their Tim Horton's coffee. Mothers wrapped in old blan-
kets from their cars will sit in the stands with other mothers or stand
inside by the coffee and hot chocolate canteen. The following food is sold
in arenas: coffee, lukewarm tea, boiling hot chocolate, fries, low-quality
nacho chips with a side of melted artificial cheese, candy and slushies
(blue or red). The latter is generally reserved for players after a good
game or practice. Parents also carry a supply of quarters for the candy
machines and hockey card machines that are sometimes the only food
for miles when the canteen is closed.

Traditional topics of conversation for dads by the glass are: how big
are the players, where did they play last year, who is 'hitting,' who is a
puck-hog, who has speed, or what is the new coach is looking for? During
regular season, those same conversations often extend to: Who is on
whose line? How much ice time is each player getting? Is anyone 'rid-
ing the pine' (or being benched)? (Or, are some players getting more
ice time than others?) And, which line should be on for a power play or
power kill? It is generally accepted that the first line on the ice is the
best line, or the 'power play' line, the forward line the team counts on to
score. There is a 'fourth line' in hockey, traditionally reserved for rough-
er players, but that tradition is very controversial and frowned upon.[205]

Mothers tend to concentrate on the relationships on and off the ice:
who is friends with whom, who the coach knows, who the coach's wife
hangs out with, which player has grown the most, who said what, when,
about whom, or which player(s) is amazing? As the season progresses,
the conversations become more focused on a single game or play or practice drill; an injury, concussion, or dryland workout routine between ice
times. But one thing is for sure: every single parent there wants their

---

205 See Chapter 4.

son or daughter to feel the heady power of victory – for themselves, and for the team as a single, solid unit. The conversations that take place during the 90-minute practices and games evolve the understanding of the team as a unit and family. These community conversations grow the reputation and image of a player, and grow the bond between the families and team players.

Patrick Roy's father Michel said that there are ten species of hockey parents:

1. "The vigilante doesn't follow the game; he studies the referee so he can bellyache about the way the game is being officiated: 'Hey, ref, you're missing a good game!'

2. The screamer hollers about everything: the game, the referee, the linesmen, the opponents, the coaches, the clock, and so on.

3. The instigator tries to provoke the opposing team's parents, insults rival players and incites his son to violence in subtle terms like, 'Smash him! Hit him! Kill him!'

4. The worrywart only has eyes for his son and is mortally afraid something terrible is going to happen to him.

5. The loser pushes his son to the limit, hoping to realize his own boyhood dreams through his son.

6. The stoic observes the game poker-faced.

7. The analyst gives us the benefit of his expertise through the contest, much to our exasperation.

8. The specialist 'coaches' from the stands and has a solution for everything.

9. The accountant spends his time calculating his son's ice time.

10. The whiner takes a very narrow view of things; the pen-

alties his son's team gets are never deserved and the other team's infractions, are never punished." [206]

Tanner has known most of these parents and players for several seasons now. For these families, the topic of conversation now surrounds who will stay in hockey beyond this year. Bantam major (the grade 9/age 14 year) is a final year of hockey for many Canadian players. At age 15, male players begin their last year of minor before being drafted into an OHL or a semi-professional team. Following this year for Tanner, he will decide: Do I stay with hockey and try to invest in my development as a career player? Or do I begin a new course in life? Do I want to go to university? Where will my future with this be? For a player who has spend 4-5 days a week, 2-3 hours a day, for the past seven years, committed to on-ice and dry land skill development, it is difficult to imagine life without it. It is difficult to say goodbye to those life-long friendships, and sometimes even more difficult for parents whose children decide to leave the sport, because, in some cases, the parents have been just as committed, if not more, to the future goal of an elite athlete or a professional hockey life. "Parents are duty bound to help their children realize their dreams and not the reverse."[207]

To an outsider this might seem obsessive, but if you think of it, the same dedication to a single long-shot could be said of the high school student who studies every night and on weekends to get into an ivy-league university, or about an entrepreneur who spends nights and weekends networking, going out, saving money to make the connections s/he needs to build a business. It is rare to balk at that commitment for the latter two, but not uncommon to hear people state that, '[sport] is a waste of time'. Why should one objective or discipline be more valued than another?

Whether one is an athlete or a mathlete, the dedication to craft still requires time, money, commitment and a great deal of family-community support to raise the elite. It is this dedication, that is rare, but wonderful when witnessed.

---

206 Michel Roy, *Patrick Roy: Winning Nothing Else* (Mississauga, ON: John Wiley & Sons Canada, Ltd., 2007), 56.
207 Ibid., 41.

New Season and a Sore Start

If you're a hockey player, everything else in between hockey seasons is either fitness training or killing time. So it is with soccer in our household. After spring tryouts are over in May, our boys usually play soccer. The weather is nice, there's lots of running involved for fitness, and at $45 (including a free jersey, socks and shorts), the price is right! I laugh when they mail me a receipt for the childrens' fitness tax credit. We surpass our taxable credits for the year in two weeks of hockey.

A lot of the soccer players on the boys' teams are hockey players too, so it's interesting to see how different, or frustrating, soccer is in Canada for coaches. In soccer, for example, the off-side is based upon the last defender. And the keeper has a huge area, or crease, but they all stick 'close to the pipes' because they are so use to the rink. The sheer size of the soccer field is difficult for hockey players too, since they've spent their last nine months inside a 200' X 85' space, and now it's double that size at 360' X 240' with all of these extra players, and no boards!

My boys always play a completely different position than they would on the ice. The older ones play defense and keeper and Jake plays striker, which he loves. Two glorious months out of the net just running. I think because of their level of fitness during the year, they excel at soccer, and do well.

Just before coming back to hockey for his first season with the Grizzlies, Jake strained his left back leg. He didn't notice it on the field, or walking or skating, but as soon as he went down for that first butterfly save, he yelped. When he came off of the ice, I could tell something was wrong. 'Did they say something mean to him?' I thought, 'Does he feel friendless?'

I looked at him questioningly, then we he got into the car, and no longer needing to save face, he started crying. His would have felt comfortable telling his old coach something was wrong without worrying about jeopardizing his pecking order on the team, but this was a new coach that he didn't yet trust. Was being injured a sign of weakness?

"I hurt myself," he said in between tears.

"Where?" I said.

"Here," he said pointing to his upper back leg, "every time I go down for a butterfly, it kills."

I stopped behind the arena for some snow, we wrapped it in a plastic bag and Jake sat on it the rest of the way home.

I hoped a night of rest and massage would do it, but the next day it was worse. This time, Jake walked off the ice half way through practice and

I have never seen him do that before.

"Well," I said, "it's not broken, but I guess you're just going to have to rest it for a few days, no hockey."

Jake starts crying.

"I know it's not how you wanted to start with a new team, but what can you do? What if it gets worse?"

I talk to my husband that evening and we decide that a steady dose of ice, massage, rest and stretching are in order. We don't have a family doctor yet, and all of the massage therapists in the area are booked up until the end of the month, so the 13-year-old who can't sit still will just have to heal at home.

The neighbor tells me that there is a woman who is amazing deep-muscle masseuse, but she only does yoga classes now. She gives me her number, and I call later that evening.

"Hello? You don't know me, but I live around the corner, we just moved in, and Mrs. Barter said you use to do massage?"

"I did," the voice on the other end says, "but I gave my table away years ago."

"Well," I persist, "You see, I-have-a-son-who-plays-hockey and he's-strained-a-muscle and really needs a-deep-muscle-massage-to-work-it-out, but-I-can't-find-anyone-else, would you be able to help us?"

"Okay, sure, bring him around tomorrow morning. I can work on him on the floor I guess. Kids are good that way," she says good-naturedly.

The next morning, we meet her and she 'goes to work'. Jake's not at all reserved about stripping down to his shorts and letting someone knead into all of his muscles. In fact, I think he enjoys it!

"Ahhhh," he moans. What a ham!

"I can tell he plays sports," she says, "he's so tight ... everywhere!"

She won't take any money for the service, so we give her a bottle of wine and a huge 'thank you!' instead.

Jake feels better afterwards, but we still ice before bed. They're first pre-season game is tomorrow, and although he may not be playing, I don't want it injured again ... just in case he goes in.

Regular Season Month 1:

Team Assessment Fee
+ 860km
+ Subway/Tim's

Total: $1,677.50

Conclusion

The families of elite hockey athletes in Canada spend a great deal of time on the road and in discussion about hockey (and local teams) at the rink. It is not unlike having a second full-time job, consuming on average, twenty hours a week in travel, practices and games for the whole family (not just the goalie or player). Siblings of elite players, who don't play themselves, may find themselves hanging around ice rinks and doing their homework on the road, or playing with the siblings of other players while they wait. Siblings, and parents, have to give up time at home visiting with friends or socializing in their own 'worlds' outside of hockey. In addition, the players themselves forego social lives outside of the sport. University athletes often say that they are either studying or practicing, and on weekends, they are on the road for games and tournaments. While other university students are going out to clubs or parties, elite athletes do not have time in their schedules for that kind of life. Their team is their society.

For elite players who try to participate in other sports, getting injured off-ice buys them time on the bench. One of Jake's team mates injured a wrist playing basketball for his school, for example, and even after the wrist was healed, the coach was still angry for the 'lack of commitment' shown, and benched him for two weeks. Many elite midget-level coaches forbid their players from partaking in any other sport. Midget is the junior qualifying year, and the pressure to succeed (for both coaches and players) is intense. And yet, the living knowledge of work ethic and 'what it takes to succeed' is a valuable commodity.

Such a level of year-round support and dedication to the task of learning and developing the skills of an elite athlete in the game of hockey become an important part of the community's collective knowledge and expertise for those that succeed. There are 'positions'[208] for every person connected to the team, not just the players on the team. Hence, when a local hockey player moves on to a career in hockey, or to play at the national level, like international champions Cassie Campbell-Pascal or T. J. Brodie, the entire community celebrates their success. Peripheral people connected to the investment in that player's triumph feel as if

---

208 Or personas.

it is their success as well. A small, skate-sharpening shop in Chatham, Ontario, for example, is proud to let people know that pro goalie, Joseph Raaymakers, still comes home to get his skates sharpened the way he likes.

'It takes a village to raise a child'; and it takes a country to raise a sport.

Average AAA Season Total per Player:

Registration
+ Assesments
+ 9 months Travel Expenses
+ Equiptment
+ Fast Food
+ Clinics
+ Gifts for Helpers

Total: <u>$21,158.41</u>p.a.

CHAPTER SIX:
All This Useless Junk

"Cards aren't really a hallmark of childhood anymore; they're a way for collectors to return to it"[209]

Surely all those old hockey magazines and aging jerseys in basements, closets and other makeshift storage spaces are useless. They must be. What are they good for? Anything? Yet hockey collectibles must offer something to people. Otherwise, why would hobbyists spend their precious time and hard-earned money gathering and taking meticulous care of their memorabilia? And what does all of this say about Canada's hockey collectibles market?

There are eight general phases of collecting, including "deciding to collect, gathering information, planning and courtship, hunting, acquisition, post-acquisition, display, and then repeating the cycle."[210] In this chapter I discuss the phenomenon of hockey memorabilia and the collector's psyche. While many different sports inspire people to seek out and accumulate collectibles of one sort or another – ranging from ticket stubs and game programs to replica jerseys and game-used equip-

---

209 Dave Jamieson, *Mint Condition: How Baseball Cards Became an American Obsession* (New York, NY: Grove Press, 2010), 9.
210 Catherine Carey, "Modeling Collecting Behavior: The Role of Set Completion." *Journal of Economic Psychology*, 29 (2008): 339.

ment – hockey is particularly interesting because in Canada it is not only associated with feelings of nostalgia, and the desire to acquire and possess—but it is also tied to notions of patriotism. After all, the linking of hockey to national identity and pride is promoted by a variety of corporate Goliaths, such as Tim Hortons and Canadian Tire, along with the Royal Canadian Mint. While ice hockey may not be mentioned in Canada's national anthem, its presence in the country has been pervasive and enduring.[211]

Yet what can we say about the hockey collectibles trade, a market that contributes to North America's healthy $12 billion sports merchandise trade?[212] What compels hockey fans to collect? According to economics theorist, Catherine Carey, motivations for collecting include "Novelty, nostalgia, notoriety, and aesthetics."[213] To discuss the phenomenon of hockey memorabilia and collector's perspective, three questions need to be asked: What do people collect? What drives them to collect? What do these things tell us about both the phenomenon of hockey collecting and Canada itself? To explore these questions, I have organized this chapter into the following three segments: (1) *Collecting is a Communal Activity,* (2) *Seduced by Nostalgia,* and (3) *The Thrill of the Hunt and Joy of Ownership.* Each section opens with a personal vignette, a composite narrative that has been formed from an experience I had over a decade ago.

Collecting is a Communal Activity

Many years ago I went to a sports collectibles show with two of my younger cousins. At the time I was a young parent in my early 30s and my first daughter was a toddler. My cousins, Doug and Dave, love to play and watch different sports, mostly hockey and baseball.

In the 1980s, my cousins and I played games of road hockey, watched hockey games, and kept up with the latest trades and standings. Doug and I revered the Montréal Canadiens, as man of our relatives had supported the team since its glorious heyday of the 1950s. Being slightly older than Doug, I vaguely recall the late 1970s Montréal dynasty, which included such artisans as Guy Lafleur. Both of us fondly remem-

---

211 See, for instance, Stephen Smith, *Puckstruck: Distracted, Delighted and Distressed by Canada's Hockey Obsession* (Vancouver, BC: Greystone Books, 2014).

212 See Mike Ozanian, "Manning Lawsuit Could Rattle $1.5 Billion Sports Memorabilia Business," *Forbes,* January 30 2014. Accessed July 15 2015. http://www.forbes.com/sites/mikeozanian/2014/01/30/manning-lawsuit-will-rattle-12-billion-dollar-sports-memorabilia-business/.

213 Carey, "Modelling Collecting Behavior," 340.

ber the surprising the Stanley Cup victories of 1986 and 1993. As time has passed, we have stayed with *Les Canadiens*, and every time our team gets eliminated from the NHL playoffs the excitement of the season and possibility of a championship is sadly extinguished.

On this particular Friday evening, Doug, Dave and I battled rain and wind, venturing from our respective homes to the airport hotel district. The hotel itself was a buzzing midsized, mid-priced facility, catering to travelers in need of a place to stay on their way in or out of the city. The hotel was also designed to host a variety of events in its multipurpose rooms. It was a tidy hotel, tidy and convenient.

After parking my van, I found my cousins waiting for me in the hotel lobby. We cheerfully greeted one another, as it had been a few months since we had last seen each other. After some casual conversation and family updates Doug pointed across the lobby to "Ballroom A"—the multipurpose room where the collectibles show was to be held. Eagerly, we strolled across the lobby, through the doorway, and into the room. Although the room was spacious, it was crowded, and was bustling with activity.

At approximately 10,000 square feet, "Ballroom A" offered a capacity of nearly 1000 people with dimensions of about 85 by 120 feet. It is used for a variety of purposes. In a given week, it could be filled with workers from a computer company on a Monday and Tuesday, an autoworker's union on a Wednesday and Thursday, and a large wedding party on a Friday. Over a given weekend, the vast room could house a large event. Of course, on this chilly November Friday, the room was hosting a sports collectibles show. In preparation of the event, the roomhad been filled with foldaway tables, neatly arranged into long rows and along the walls. Behind each table stood a seller – almost exclusively white men – and these vendors were many things—peddlers, collectors, investors, and entrepreneurs.

The tables were jam packed with various vintage and newly produced memorabilia. While some items were placed directly on the tables, the more valuable ones were safely tucked away (yet still visible) in display cases. Select few items were hockey artifacts from the distant past, such as old game programs, newspapers, and Bee Hive photos. Other items were newer and shinier, such as special issue coins and figurines. At every table was an assortment of hockey cards, with many of the iconic player cards (the Wayne Gretzkys, Gordie Howes, and Bobby Orrs) lovingly placed in protective cases. The wide range of items on display varied in condition from poor to pristine. Between these peddler stalls were pathways, circuits crowded with collectors, young and old—prevalently male. It was at once a large assemblage of museum-like artifacts and a bustling makeshift indoor marketplace.

My cousins and I strode into the room in a state of great anticipation. We had planned this evening months earlier, researching the various dates, locations and sizes of sports collectibles shows in and around the city. We had all looked forward to spending time together, and perhaps meeting some of the vendors and shoppers. The three of us lived in different parts of the Greater Toronto area, and our busy schedules prevented us from regularly seeing one another.

"Let's first step through all of the aisles before buying anything," I suggested.

"Sounds great. What are you looking for?" Doug asked.

"Books."

"Books?" Dave asked in disbelief. "You won't find books here!"

"What sort of books?" Doug inquired. "Autographed ones?

"No, I'm looking for player guidebooks."

"You mean like the magazines that come out before the season starts?" Doug asked.

"Sort of. When I was young we didn't have season forecaster magazines. There was no such thing back then. They used to come out as pocket books."

Doug grinned. "Yes, you are pretty ancient."

"The books in this series came out in the late 60s, 70s, and early to mid-80s."

"And I take it you used to have them?"

"I used to have four—but over the years I lost them."

"And that's what you're looking for?"

"Not exactly. I've replaced all the ones I lost, and I've bought some others as well—ones I never had before. Actually, I've even picked up a few that were published before I was born."

"Where did you find them?"

"Well, you can't get them in used bookshops anymore. I've had to go to online shops."

"And you really think you'll find them here?"

"If these books are in Toronto they're all either up for sale on online bookshops, or they're at shows like this." I paused and then smiled. "Either that, or they're in someone's collection and not for sale."

"Heaven forbid!" Doug laughed.

"I don't think you'll find them here," Dave concluded. "It's not like you're looking for cards."

"And it sounds like they're pretty old," Doug agreed.

Dave smiled. "You should get cards," he advised. "I honestly don't think you'll find those old books here."

"But there are a lot of older things at these shows," I countered. "Who knows?"

"But who buys vintage books at a sports collectibles show? It's mostly jerseys, cards, and toys—things like that."

Pausing for a moment I thought about this. I knew my cousin was right. Yet I remained hopeful. "We'll see," I replied.

The above vignette provides a glimpse into the social aspect of hockey collecting. Acquiring hockey memorabilia straddles two levels of community. On a smaller scale, it straddles the local community—which involves personally interacting with other hockey enthusiasts. On a larger scale, it is a nation-wide interest—perhaps because the sport itself is often seen as a mythical, 'nation-building,' pseudo-religious phenomenon.

The Local Community

Hockey collectors interact at the local level. They gather in person and meet online to talk about what they collect. Whether it is cards, programs, ticket stubs, coins, magazines, newspapers, pennants, jerseys, t-shirts, etc.—collectors talk to collectors. After all, they have a shared passion. They also have a perceived shared history. Sometimes collectors consult one another to learn more about an item (or set) they are interested in (or are already) collecting. Other times, they chat with one another about a game, player, team, or bygone era. If hockey fandom is a form of culture, then the hockey collecting community is a narrower sphere of that culture. And hockey collectors have various outlets to interact within this dynamic.

Online Community - On the sprawling Internet there is a wide array of websites, discussion boards, and marketplaces where individuals can talk about hockey in general and collecting more specifically.[214] Because people may collect very precise items (such as hockey card wrappers from the 1970s), they may need to go online to find others who are interested in – or even know about – the item set they are seeking. In fact, there may not even be someone else who collects the same item set in the same city or town. While these collectors may certainly enjoy sitting down with other hobbyists at a shop or collectibles show, their collection-oriented research and dialogue may be most conveniently served online.

Collectibles Shops - In cities and towns across Canada, sports and memorabilia shops act as both shopping destinations and hubs for the collecting community. Decades ago, Comics Unlimited/Sports Connection was one such hub. Located in a small plaza at the corner of Bathurst and Eglinton in Toronto, the shop had a small television where games and sports talk shows were perpetually on air. Whether it was the early afternoon or early evening one of the owners would always be at the front of the shop holding court with a gaggle of sports fans discussing the latest trade or rumor. These sorts of shops were once a destination, a place to buy things, an informal sort of art gallery, and a social gathering space. Comics Unlimited/Sports Connection eventually packed up shop and moved to the suburbs before closing in the early 2000s. Other collectible hubs, such as the once popular Legends of the Game – located in Toronto's theatre district – have reduced their size and/or diversified their content over time. The once vast shop, now named From Hockey to Hollywood, is presently half its former size. Like the revolving door of hockey arenas, sports shops have contributed to the ever-shifting identity and culture of cities and towns across Canada. As anthropologist Anouk Bélanger notes: "The 'work' of memory around these places or buildings in a continuously changing time-space matrix can offer a window into the continuously changing cultures of cities."[215] While sports memorabilia shops have gradually disappeared, the hockey collectibles show has become a staple from coast to coast.

Collectibles Shows - As collectors have transferred their shopping hab-

---

214 A popular Internet hub for hockey dialogue is HFBoards. There are many forums and threads on this discussion board, and the number of posts (as of July 10 2015 exceeded 60 million). Accessed July 10, 2015. http://hfboards.hockeysfuture.com/.
215 Anouk Bélanger, "Urban Space and Collective Memory," *Canadian Journal of Urban Research*, 11:1 (2002), 71.

its and social interactions from bricks and mortar shops to online stores and auction sites, the sports collectibles show has emerged as a murky in-between place – where many online sellers fleetingly set up shop on a habitual basis at temporary marketplaces. Monthly and biweekly (or even annually or biannually) collectible shows are held in and around cities and towns across Canada. It is at the shows that collectors now indulge in their face-to-face meetings and discussions. These shows provide a place to meet with others, and a venue to look over (and perhaps even touch) a wide variety of hockey memorabilia. While collectors buy many items online, there is something to be said for the experience of physically holding an item and discussing it with the seller before making a purchase. The people who staff the tables at a collectibles show are often knowledgeable and genuinely interested in hockey. They know about the history of the game and have specific knowledge about their favorite teams, players and eras. They also know – and have strong opinions – about rule changes, trades, the design of jerseys, and various hockey products. In some regards, the sports collectibles show is like an academic conference – where the memorabilia peddlers come prepared to engage in conversation about many different general or specific topics. At this local level, hockey collecting is a social activity where people meet with one another and revel in discussing a variety of things relating to the sport and to their collections.

Secondary Market - While the sports collectibles show and shop act as a social hub, they are also the manifestation of the collectibles economic market. When objects are produced and initially sold, they represent a primary market – and when people become interested in acquiring previously owned objects, a *secondary market* emerges.[216] This secondary market facilitates the buying-and-selling of used hockey memorabilia. It is the economic community which collectors experience at the local level as they interact with others and build their collectible empires. According to Carey, "A community associated with the collectible raises the social value of the collection"[217] "A well developed community," in Carey's view, "will assign value to certain standards for the collectible (e.g., size, generations, weight, etc.), assign value to the authentication standards (condition, grading scales, etc.), support investment value (by providing collector's guides and a more stable market for resale), and

---

216 Carey, "Modelling Collecting Behavior."
217 Ibid., 339.

create a social network with other collectors (through online discussion boards, conferences and trade shows, club memberships, etc.)."[218] It is a full-fledged market economy. How else could a small blue piece of cardboard bearing the image of Wayne Gretzky be sold for $94,000?[219] In terms of belonging and status, a collectible "community provides a sense of social acceptance of the collector and his or her collection."[220]

The National Community

Hockey is a part of Canada's constructed mythology. It is pervasive. Of course, these ideas are nothing new – and have been discussed in such books as the Ken Dryden and Roy MacGregor's bestselling *Home Game* (1990), Brian Kennedy's *My Country is Hockey* (2011) and Paul Henderson and Jim Prime's *How Hockey Explains Canada* (2011).[221] Over the years hockey's image and surrounding aura have been reshaped and molded to fit the changing times.[222] Folktales dating from the early 1900s tell stories of acrobatic rovers deking through opponents to score backwards goals and rugged workhorses trekking through blizzards to beat the first drop of the puck.[223]

These folktales shifted into shared experiences on national radio broadcasts in the 1930s, which eventually paved the way for the Canadian Broadcasting Corporation (CBC) to start nationally televising broadcasts on Saturday nights in 1952.[224] "[T]he cultural association of hockey and Canada," according to religion scholar Denis J. Bekkering, "is not natural but constructed, and government efforts to link the two began in earnest during a period when the nation was wrestling with

---

218 Ibid., 339.

219 To read story behind this exemplar of exorbitant hockey card transactions, see Andrew Tolentino, "Gretzky Rookie Nabs More Than $94,000," *Beckett Media*, May 2 2011. Accessed July 15, 2015. http://www.beckett.com/news/2011/05/gretzky-rookie-nabs-more-than-94000/.

220 Carey, "Modeling Collecting Behavior," 339.

221 See Ken Dryden and Roy MacGregor, Home Game: *Hockey and Life in Canada* (Toronto, ON: McClelland & Stewart, 1990), Brian Kennedy, *My Country is Hockey: How Hockey Explains Canadian Culture, History, Politics, Heroes, French-English Rivalry,* and *Who We Are as Canadians* (Edmonton, AB: Argenta, 2011), and Paul Henderson with Jim Prime, *How Hockey Explains Canada: The Sport that Defines a Country* (Chicago, IL: Triumph Books, 2011).

222 Paul W. Bennett, "A Family Squabble: What's Behind the Quest for Genesis in the Canadian Hockey World?" in *Putting it on Ice: Proceedings of the 2012 Hockey Conference*, edited by Lori Dithurbide and Colin Howell (2012): 32-33. Accessed July 15, 2015. http://www.smu.ca/campus-life/putting-it-on-ice-proceedings.html.

223 See Paul Quarrington (Editor), *Original Six: True Stories from Hockey's Classic Era* (Toronto, ON: Reed Books Canada, 1996), and Eric Whitehead, *Cyclone Taylor: A Hockey Legend* (Toronto, ON: Doubleday Canada, 1977).

224 See Michael McKinley, *Hockey Night in Canada: 60 Seasons* (Toronto, ON: Viking, 2012).

its public connection to the transcendent" – the 1960s.[225] It was a decade when Canada was designing its flag, preparing to host the 1967 World Expo, struggling with the Quiet Revolution and genesis of the Separatist Movement, and removing a number of its racial barriers to immigration.[226] Suffice to say, hockey is a national symbol in Canada. Yet it remains one that has been artificially constructed and reconstructed through the years.

National Phenomenon - Over 22 million Canadians witnessed Sidney Crosby's game-winning goal in the 2010 Vancouver Winter Olympics. It was the most watched event in Canadian history. Whether it is the Stanley Cup finals, the Winter Olympics, or the latest Junior Championship, hockey events are seen as (and indeed become) shared memories among Canadians. Because hockey is perceived as a unifying force, it becomes a 'connector' for those who are drawn into the sport. It is a nation-wide pastime, and accordingly, collecting hockey memorabilia is a national phenomenon.

Some collectors may be inclined to equate hockey nationalism and the sport itself with an idyllic activity, emblematic of quiet communities that are at once welcoming, safe and innocent. Of course, hockey is also treated as a mythical, pseudo-religious force – and at its core, the game is seen as something that is distinctly Canadian. It is "more than a national passion," sports researchers Greg Ramshaw and Tom Hinch astutely observe.[227] Hockey is perceived as "an essential part of being Canadian; a cultural identifier that separates Canadians from all others."[228] Collecting hockey memorabilia is thus a local activity that is entwined with a larger national community.

Pseudo-Religion - As a national sport, hockey is also seen as having spiritual qualities. Over the years, various mystical sites, miracle events, and relics have attained a degree of national awareness – and it is unsur-

---

225 Denis J. Bekkering, "Of 'Lucky Loonies': and 'Golden Pucks': Canadian Hockey Relics and Civil Religiosity," *Studies in Religion*, 44:1 (2015): 59.
226 While much has been written about Canada's changing political and social landscape in the 1960s, two useful articles include: Julia Lalande, "The Roots of Multiculturalism – Ukranian-Canadian involvement in the Multiculturalism Discussion of the 1960s as an Example of the Position of the 'Third Force,'" *Canadian Ethnic Studies*, 38:1 (2006): 47-64 and Harold Troper, "Canada's Immigration Policy Since 1945," *International Journal*, 48:2 (1993): 255-281.
227 Greg Ramshaw and Tom Hinch, "Place Identity and Sport Tourism," *Current Issues in Tourism*, 9:4&5 (2006): 404.
228 Ibid.

prising that certain sites have been promoted as national destinations. The Hockey Hall of Fame (HHOF) – located Toronto's financial district – is at once a museum, a vault, and a cathedral. Navigating the various pathways and corridors of the Hall – with their overflowing hockey artifacts and endless interactive possibilities – eventually leads fans to a dimly lit high-ceilinged room that houses the hallowed Stanley Cup. High above the Cup is a stained-glass dome reminiscent of the cathedrals of medieval Europe. While not all collectors are necessarily moved by the pseudo-religious aura hockey seems to exude, some certainly are. After all, hockey collectibles are often seen as relics of Canada's national pastime – and Lucky Loonies exemplify this sort of thinking.

In 2002 the Canadian men's hockey team captured the gold medal at the Winter Olympics for the first time in half a century. Buried beneath center ice was a $1 coin (called a loonie), which had been carefully placed there by a superstitious Canadian worker.[229] This loonie has come to be known as the 'lucky loonie' and it is now on display in the HHOF. Because the lucky loonie has come to personify a spectacular moment in Canada's history – and capture a notion of 'Canadian exceptionalism' – hockey fans across the country have been encouraged to make a 'pilgrimage' to the Hall to touch the celebrated coin. As religion scholar Denis J. Bekkering noted, however, "The opportunity to touch the coin attracted a flood of visitors, resulting in the rapid deterioration of the Lucky Loonie's golden patina, and the decision of Hall officials to cover it with a clear plastic disc."[230] Consequently, visitors can now only gaze at the coin and touch the casing that protects it. The legendary coin itself – like Michaeangelo's Pieta – is securely protected from the prying hands of tourists behind a see-through shield. Journeying to the HHOF to be near the Lucky Loonie (and other such artifacts) is seen as an act of patriotism *and* spiritualism.[231] Aware of the pseudo-religious sea of emotions associated with hockey, the Royal Canadian Mint and hockey arena owners have leapt into the collectibles market.

Minting Coins and Auctioning Memories - In 2004, two years after the mythical tale of the lucky loonie, Canada's "Mint trademarked the phrase "Luckey Loonie" to describe a new dollar coin produced in an-

---

229 Introduced in 1987, a one-dollar coin is known in Canada as a 'loonie' because it depicts a loon on one side. See Bekkering, "Of 'Lucky Loonies' and 'Golden Pucks.'"
230 Ibid., 62.
231 Ibid., 61.

ticipation of that year's Olympic Games in Athens, Greece."[232] In short order, demand for the loonie rose by 62 percent, and the ever-expanding collectibles business suddenly opened a variety of possibilities for the Crown Corporation.[233] In addition to marketing special lines of circulated money, the Mint has produced a variety of uncirculated Olympic coins designed (and priced) for those who have more capital to spend on their hobby. In this unique intersection of nationalism, business, and memorabilia, Canada's Mint, "a government-owned corporation, engaged in the production and distribution of its own, purportedly powerful, civil religious relic replicas."[234] Yet the Mint is not alone in the peddling of memory trinkets.

When well-known arenas – mystical sites, such as Montréal's Forum and Toronto's Maple Leaf Gardens – were replaced with newer homes, the old buildings were stripped down, broken up, and sold to collectors. These auctions were full blown affairs. In the words of Bélanger, Montréal 1996 auction was an event where hockey fans, collectors, and "ghosts were forced to look on during a public auction at which the Forums seats and other memorabilia were literally ripped from the building."[235] Interestingly, people have not only sought out the various artifacts on offer at these auctions, but some have even collected the glossy catalogues produced for the events. While collecting catalogues may be further removed from the game, it is far more affordable than collecting arena and game-used artifacts themselves.

Hockey collecting is a community activity and space – on a local and national level. This community is at once a perception and a reality. In part, collecting memorabilia leads hockey fans to interact and form bonds with others. On another level, collecting hockey memorabilia is perceived as an act of patriotism, and one's collectibles can be viewed as a link to national history (hockey events) and the nation itself (which is partly defined by its passion for the sport). Whether or not collecting truly is a patriotic act is immaterial. It is the perception that shapes the motives, actions, and lived reality of collectors and fans. While 22 million Canadians watched Sidney Crosby's Olympic gold-winning goal on TV, one wonders how many of those viewers wish they had some sort of artifact to remember (and connect them to) that moment of 'Canadian

---

232 Ibid.
233 Ibid.
234 Ibid., 70.
235 Ibid., 70.

exceptionalism.' Yet hockey collecting is not purely about the here and the now—it is also about the past. More precisely, it is about bringing an imagined past into the present.

Seduced by Nostalgia

My cousins and I stepped through the aisles for well over an hour. With so many people at the event we were forced to take a leisurely pace as we strolled from table to table, taking stock of the artifacts that were up for sale. During our initial walk through the congested pathways, we refrained from purchasing anything. We refrained from even attempting to negotiate with sellers. Instead, we quietly surveyed what people had on offer as well as what they were asking for their assortment of bric-a-bracs.

Like any market, the prices displayed at a sports collectibles show are not firm. Rather, they are negotiable—as buyers delicately balance their desire to get the best price without putting off the sellers. It is an atmosphere that promotes haggling. Yet before engaging in any sort of haggling, my cousins and I needed to get a sense of what sellers were offering as well as what they were asking.

The set of books I was collecting at the time was published between 1968 and 1985. Jim Proudfoot, a *Toronto Star* sportswriter wrote and edited the series. During the series run, a new guidebook came out every year. Each book was set up the same way, with chapters organized by team. Each chapter opened with a team roster, which was followed by a set of snappy player narratives, representing about one-third of the team's roster. Written in a conversational style, these biographies were updated every year, as the players' careers and lives unfolded. It was as though each player's career was an individual hockey narrative, and these narratives collectively formed a part of the larger ongoing saga of the National Hockey League (NHL) itself.

I had four of the Jim Proudfoot guidebooks when I was in elementary school. Specifically, I had the books from 1982 to 1985. As I think about those four books, I remember paging through them when I was young. They joined me on camping trips and followed me to school. Other times, I flipped through a guidebook while watching a Saturday night game of *Hockey Night in Canada*. A couple of times I even took a guidebook to a game—on one of the handful of occasions I went to Maple Leaf Gardens. Those four reliable books were well worn and much cherished. Yet somewhere between my late teens and early thirties I mislaid them.

Years later I had a moment where I wanted to peruse those books, and after searching stacks of milk crates in my basement I realized I had lost them. With my original copies of the Jim Proudfoot guidebooks gone forever, I turned to the Internet in my disappointment. Searching various used book and hockey collectible websites I was quickly able to find information about the Jim Proudfoot player guidebooks, easily obtaining images of book covers. I learned how many books were published in total, and further researched the series by going to collector websites reading different fans' narratives about owning or collecting the books.

It was a niche market to be certain, but a market nevertheless. While I was unable to find any copies of the books as I scouted the larger used bookshops and thrift stores in and around the city I soon purchased copies online (on eBay.ca, abebooks.com, and amazon.ca).

As my cousins and I strolled around the marketplace, my eyes darted around those crowded tables in search of the Proudfoot books. I was excited to examine each aisle, and every table presented new possibilities of finding books that I dearly wanted. It was an opportunity to scavenge around a vast market and potentially haggle with sellers. In the end, if I were to find any books to add to my collection, I would always associate them with the evening I spent with my cousins at the collectibles show—as every collectible has its own narrative, and a part of that narrative is the story behind 'the purchase.' The sports collectibles show was, in many ways, an experience of nostalgia. I was spending time with family and revisiting my youth.

My experience at the sports show was rooted in memories and a link to the past. Like many other collectors, I was motivated by a sense of nostalgia. Hockey collectors sometimes seek out (or keep) such things as hockey cards and ticket stubs—objects that harken from their youth. Collecting hockey memorabilia is connected to a sense of local and national community, and it is also tied to the past. Intrinsically, collectors are driven by an inner desire to revisit, reconstruct, and possibly even reimagine their past. Extrinsically, those who produce hockey memorabilia today create objects with the intent of fostering a sense of nostalgia as they tap into memories of collectors. Yet what is nostalgia?

Nostalgia is both an idea and an emotion. In a state of nostalgia, the past is revisited, reconstructed, and possibly even brought into the present.[236] There is an illusory aspect to nostalgia, which "typically conjures up images of a previous time when life was 'good.'"[237] Originally seen as a physical condition, "Swiss physician Johannes Hofer coined the term in the late seventeenth century to refer to the extreme homesickness that Swiss mercenaries experienced."[238] In today's context, nostalgia is seen as a bridge that "may give us a key to the gate connecting the lessons of the past to the needs of the present."[239] Through nostalgic practices – such as collecting hockey artifacts – "Memory is always being reconstructed in the present context."[240] Stockpiling hockey memorabilia can lead some to experience a "personal reverie" and escape (albeit temporarily) from the complications of present, such as pressures at work.[241] Simply put, nostalgia brings the past – a time that is lost – into the present. It is seductive.

Past Experiences

Hockey collectors access feelings of nostalgia in a variety of ways and contexts. Events (such as hockey games) and places (such as rinks) evoke feelings of nostalgia. Such feelings may involve watching a famous goal in childhood and then recalling that moment years later. A recording of that goal, a hockey card of one of the players involved in the goal, or another 'reminder' piece of memorabilia may prompt that fan to revisit the first time that goal was experienced in the distant past. Consequently, the "desire to visit sport's past may be driven by individual memory, televised rebroadcasts of famous matches, re-creations of famous sports moments on film, descriptions of class sport achievements in books, are even artwork displaying images of past sports moments."[242] It is a matter of looking back with purpose and emotion.

Remnants of the Past

Just as particular moments may evoke feelings of nostalgia, so may places

---

236 Janelle L. Wilson, "'REMEMBER WHEN...' A Consideration of the Concept of Nostalgia," *ETC: A Review of General Semantics*, 56:3 (1999): 296-304.
237 Ibid., 297.
238 Ibid.
239 Ibid., 303.
240 Bélanger, "Urban Space and Collective Memory," 82.
241 Wilson, "'REMEMBER WHEN...'," 301.
242 Ramshaw and Hinch, "Place Identity and Sport Tourism," 399-400.

themselves—such as a hall of fame, or a hockey arena. Perhaps because nostalgia is such a powerful force, the HHOF is at once a memorabilia mecca—a cathedral, a vault, and an advertisement. It plays "a strategic role in the public remembering and interpretation of sports"—hockey in particular.[243] Hockey rinks and arenas can also be symbols of nostalgia. As such, "the prospective closing of the Montréal Forum [in 1996] in favour of a new, high-tech arena created an uproar of reactions in the city and launched an unprecedented wave of nostalgic sentiments."[244] The hallowed arena had become a place where historic events (such as memorable hockey games) unfolded and the people of the city (and province) came together as families, fans, and citizens. Consequently, "The Forum had emerged as a vital public space in Montréal. It was a commercial space, of course, but 'the people' had claimed the building symbolically over they years."[245] Unsurprisingly, legions of hockey fans flocked to the building to purchase artifacts when they went on the auction block. And many of those fans would have been driven by a sense of 'place nostalgia' and desire to capture and freeze moments in time. "By bidding on the banners and time clocks and the penalty box", Bélanger muses, fans and hobbyists "hoped to bottle it and take it home."[246]

For those who could not make it to one of the illustrious arena auctions, clothing companies have cultivated a throwback market, where fans can purchase jerseys that replicate the designs of yesteryear—including defunct teams and long disused logos. A perusal of the unwieldy official online shop of the NHL reveals a glittering array of vintage jerseys, ranging from the minimalist Ottawa Senators logo of the 1920s to the bright gold-and-purple LA Kings design of the 1970s and early 1980s.[247] What is never mentioned in these jersey descriptions, however, is that the Ottawa franchise moved to St. Louis in 1934 in financial disarray, and that the LA Kings was a constant financial burden to owners in its first two decades.[248] What also is not highlighted on the descriptions of the vintage jerseys is

243 Bruce Kidd, "The Making of a Hockey Artifact," *Journal of Sport History*, 23:3 (1996): 328.
244 Bélanger, "Urban Space and Collective Memory," 71.
245 Ibid.
246 Ibid., 76-77.
247 To peruse the current and throwback jerseys available at the NHL's official shop, see: http://shop.nhl.com.
248 The financial woes of many NHL franchises have been chronicled over the years. To read about the troubles of the Ottawa Senators, see Paul Kitchen, *Win, Tie, or Wrangle: The Inside Story of the Ottawa Senators* 1883-1934 (Manotick, ON: Penumbria Press, 2008). To read about the difficulties faced by the Los Angles Kings, see Stephen Brunt, *Gretzky's Tears: Hockey, Canada, and the Day Everything Changed* (Toronto, ON: Knoph Canada, 2009).

that the NHL was racially segregated its first few decades.[249] The jersey pages on the NHL's official shop presents a filtered version of history. It is also gendered. On the jersey page for the Ottawa Senators, for instance, men's jerseys outnumber women's jerseys by a count of 14 to 2.[250]

According to Stephen Andon, team jerseys "symbolize more than just a team; they can become transcendent icons that represent a city; even a country; and its enduring memories."[251] "[I]ntended for nostalgic effect," throwback jerseys have carved out a healthy segment of today's sportswear trade, where there has been a consistent "emotional reaction to retro sportswear."[252] Whether it is genuine artifacts or replica memorabilia, collectors have many choices when it comes to reveling in nostalgia. Yet it is a selective version of history that is presented, and marketed to a certain segment of the population.

Collecting and Memory

We rely on the past, and indeed use it, to make sense of our present.[253] As Bélanger notes, "Sometimes one form of memory becomes the officially sanctioned history of a given space. Historical fragments and images are fused into an imaginary unity that creates the impression of a truthful history with unavoidable lessons for the present."[254] The Lucky Loonie, inexorably linked to the 2002 Winter Olympics, exemplifies this phenomenon. And the sprawling tentacles of mass media and the magic of social construction lead to situations where some "propos[e] their memory as *the* memory."[255] Reflecting on the manifestation of hockey sites in urban spaces, Bélanger observes that: "The production of space and the production of history are both essential in constructing the conditions for the possibility of memories."[256] If hockey is (at least in part) a matter of perceived national consciousness and shared memory, then what does this say about the practice and popularity of collecting hockey memorabilia?

---

249 The first African-Canadian did not join the NHL until 1958, over four decades after the league's inaugural game. Willie O'Ree played 4 games in 1958 and 43 in 1961 for the Boston Bruins. NHL fans would not see another African-Canadian in the league until 1974, when Mike Marson made his debut with the Washington Capitals. Thus, in total, one African-Canadian played in the NHL during its first 50 years and two played in the league in its first 60 years. To read more about racial identity and hockey in Canada, see Cecil Harris, *Breaking the Ice* (Toronto, ON: Insomniac Press, 2003).
250 See http://shop.nhl.com/Ottawa_Senators_Jerseys. Accessed July 10, 2015.
251 Stephen Andon, "Rooting for the Clothes: The Materialization of Memory in Baseball's Throwback Uniforms," *NINE: A Journal of Baseball History and Culture*, 21:2 (2013): 32.
252 Ibid., 34, 41.
253 Bélanger, "Urban Space and Collective Memory."
254 Ibid., 87.
255 Ibid.
256 Ibid.

On one level, it tells us how dominant hockey is as a symbol and object of attention in Canada. It is exclusive.

Drawing from the work of Formanek and Freud, Carey notes that: "collecting behavior" can be linked to "to experiences in infancy and to relationships with other people."[257] Yet hockey collecting is not only about childhood nostalgia and belonging to a community, whether real or imagined. At times, objects of memorabilia offer fans and collectors a way to look backwards and romanticize the past—where the past is "reclaimed and represented in one-dimensional and unrealistic ways."[258]

The Thrill of the Hunt and Joy of Ownership

Strolling around the aisles with my cousins it quickly became clear that hockey books – even the vintage guidebooks I sought out – were available at the show. They were not abundant, but they were there nevertheless. While these books were available-for sale it seemed that people were not too interested in buying them. After all, items like cards and jerseys are at the epicenter of the sports collectibles landscape.

"I told you there'd be books," I proudly told my cousins.

"You did. I can't believe it." Doug agreed.

It was a pleasant surprise. "I've seen some of the guidebooks I'm looking for too," I added. "I can't wait to go back to those tables!"

It was pleasing to know that some of the books I was looking for were on sale at the show. Here I was standing in a vast room with many vendors, some of whom had very old hockey books—and they were like artifacts, which had passed through the hands of various hockey fans over the years. Who knew where those books had been, or who had once owned them? Perhaps someone long ago took one of those books to the Montréal Forum. While the books I had found were certainly not in perfect condition, there were many that would fill gaps in my collection. Splitting up, my cousins and I went on our individual memorabilia quests. I scurried back to chat with the different sellers who had books on offer. And I had three strategies in mind as I went about my task. First, I knew that if I bought multiple books at one time I would get a better deal. Second, I knew that if I went to a table multiple times I might have less leverage when negotiating a

---

257 Carey, "Modelling Collecting Behavior," 337.
258 Bélanger, "Urban Space and Collective Memory," 74.

price. Third, I knew that if I paid with cash the seller would be more open to negotiation. I knew these things from past experiences at markets. Consequently, I planned to go to a table and strike a cash-deal on the spot.

The anticipation of haggling excited me. I could not wait to start the process. Being able to interact directly with sellers and go back and forth over the price is much more enjoyable than ordering a book on the Internet where you never meet the seller or talk about the book you are buying. Buying collectibles on the Internet can be a social interaction, but it is very different than the face-to-face experience.

By the end of the evening I had bought nine books, three of which were duplicates. Over the years I have added two books to my collection of the Jim Proudfoot series and I now have seventeen of the eighteen NHL guidebooks that were published between 1968 and 1985. While I do want that last book I also realize that once I get it, my endeavor will be over.

At the end of the evening my cousins and I exited "Ballroom A" (the makeshift bustling market) in both exhaustion and exhilaration. We had all bought various collectibles (both planned and unplanned) and we had all somehow refrained from going to the hotel ATM machine during the evening. And it was in this state of weary excitement that the three of us plunked ourselves down on a hotel sofa to share our items and purchase stories with one another.

"I can't believe you found all those books," Dave admitted.

"I never thought you'd find them."

"How much were they?" Doug asked.

I opened the plastic bag I held to glance over my prize guidebooks. "The five books from 1974 to 1978 were fifteen dollars and the four from the eighties were twelve dollars," I answered.

Dave nodded. "I can't believe it," he replied in disbelief.

"I know. I got nine vintage books for less than 30 dollars. Do you know how many hours of enjoyment I will get out of these books? These are books you may not read cover-to-cover, but you can dip into any one of them anytime."

"Did you get any duplicates?" Doug inquired.

"Yes," I admitted. "Three of them are duplicates."

"And do you still need any in the series, or do you have the whole set now?"

"I still need three."

We chatted more about the evening and reminisced. We also

talked about the current hockey season that was underway, spending a disproportional amount of time reviewing and comparing the different things we had bought. After a final goodbye we went on our separate ways.

When I arrived home from the collectibles show I went into the spare bedroom we use as a sort of library and gently took out all of my Proudfoot guidebooks. I also pulled out my notebook that lists my different book collections. Flipping to the Jim Proudfoot guidebook page, I looked over the checklist and updated it, adding information on the new books I had just purchased. This page was designed as a table with five columns. There was a column for the name (issue) of the book, the purchase date, the name of seller, the price, and the condition of book. After updating my checklist, I had a closer look at the spine and corners of the new books. On a grading scale, all would be described as either fair (Fair) or good (G). For thirty-year books that had been owned by children and adolescents, this was to be expected. Turning on my computer, I went to websites that provide photos of the covers of the different guidebooks in the Proudfoot series, paying close attention to the images of the covers of the remaining three books I still did not have in my collection.

After gently flipping through my nine newly purchased books and reading the short biographies of some of my favorite players – all the while taking care not to further crack the spine or further damage any of the pages or page corners– I put all of the books back in order on the bookshelf.

While the above narrative sketch is one of community and nostalgia, it is also one of taking thrill in 'the search' and finding joy in ownership. Hockey collectors are not only driven by a desire to belong and sense of nostalgia. Some are motivated to collect individual items or sets of items because they take pleasure in the challenge of the hunt. Moreover, collectors can find joy in owning their collectibles for a variety of reasons—as collectibles have many different sorts of possible values.

Set Completion

According to Catherine Carey, "In the social psychology literature, many individuals are understood to have a natural desire to collect things for various reasons. Financial gain is only one of those reasons. Set completion is another."[259] Of course, people may collect for both reasons once. The desire to complete a set is not a simple one, and "a complete set may be worth more in the secondary market, if one exists, than the sum of those individual pieces."[260] Collectors value their memorabilia because each item has value for its "ordinary use" as well as its "aesthetic value."[261] The Jim Proudfoot books I collected, for instance, could be enjoyed as informative books and could also be enjoyed as artifacts from the past with cover art that captures a time gone by.

In the eyes of collectors, items may also have "social value" as well as value in the items "contribution to the collection."[262] When bidding on items at an auction – whether it is in person on online – It is clear to collectors that a certain community desires the objects they collect. Moreover, "The social value may simply be the individual's utility from owning the complete set (becoming closer to his or her ideal self) or it could be a collecting community's idea of the collection's financial worth on the secondary model."[263] In comparing the thinking behind collectors and non-collectors, Carey notes: "A noncollector would not value an additional unit to a collection any different than the value of the marginal unit of the good in ordinary use. A collector would place value on both the marginal unit for its ordinary use and on its contribution to the collection."[264] While the drive to complete collectible sets is not uniform; the drive itself is common in collectors.

Narrative Value

The items that people collect are tied to memories and narratives. In terms of stories, when conducting a qualitative study with collector participants, researchers Watson, Valtchanov, Hancock, and Mandryk observed that: "Narrative became an important theme throughout the interviews. The stories about an item often added to the intrinsic value"[265] The research team noted that the stories (cherished) associated with memorabilia items "could be stories about the original function, event, location, athlete, or stories that were created post-acquisition, such as getting the

---

259 Carey, "Modelling Collecting Behavior," 336.
260 Ibid.
261 Ibid., 338.
262 Ibid.
263 Ibid., 344.
264 Ibid., 338.
265 Diane Watson, Deltcho Valtchanov, Mark Handcock, and Regan Mandryk, "Designing a Gameful System to Support the Collection, Curation, Exploration, and Sharing of Sports Memorabilia," *CHIPlay'14* (2014): 451.

item signed by the athlete."[266] One participant in the study explained: "I won't buy anything off anybody if there's no story. If there's no story to it, I don't want it. Because the most important thing about it is the history of the peace, where it's come from, the route it's travelled."[267] Narrative was certainly a part of my enjoyment in seeking out and collecting the Jim Proudfoot guidebooks, as my own sketches indicate.

A number of recently published books exemplify the desire to collect (and own) objects that have their own narratives. In *Hockey Card Stories*, for instance, sports announcer Ken Reid tells the story behind 59 hockey cards from the 1970s and 1980s. Perhaps moved by a sense of nostalgia, Reid selected cards and players he enjoyed in his younger days. And as a broadcaster, he has been able to meet those 59 players depicted on the cards, and interview them about the photograph on the card, the season at hand, their hockey career, as well as their life after NHL (professional) hockey. The story behind each card is an individual one, sharing tales of rookie jinxes, faulty equipment, dated hairstyles, and uncomfortable photo sessions. Many players themselves were excited when they first learned that they were to have their own hockey card and are proud that people send them cards to be signed and sent back. Reid's 59 cards have nostalgic value, aesthetic value, and they each have narrative value. Similarly, Jon Waldman recently inventoried the stories behind hundreds of player- and team-oriented memorabilia, in *He Shoots, He Saves*.[268]

Preservation Value

The desire to own hockey memorabilia is also fuelled by the desire to preserve artifacts and prevent them from being damaged (or further damaged) or even destroyed. And the desire to collect and own is also driven by a desire to preserve, much like curators in museums and art galleries. Some collectors have a compulsion to collect items that otherwise might be thrown away and lost forever. One participant in the Watson et al. study noted: "There are many [athletes] whose contracts have never seen the light of day. What happened was those documents didn't get pulled out of the garbage, so they just got destroyed. It's very sad."[269] These objects of the past are worth preserving because of their symbolic and historic value. They tell a story and when they are gone the story is diminished, or lost.

---

266 Watson et al., "Designing a Gameful System," 451.
267 Ibid., 451.
268 Publication details for the books mentioned in this paragraph are as follows Ken Reid, *Hockey Card Stories: True Tales from Your Favourite Players* (Toronto, ON: ECW Press, 2014) and John Waldman, *He Shoots, He Saves: The Story of Hockey's Collectible Treasures* (Toronto, ON: ECW Press, 2015).
269 Watson et al., "Designing a Gameful System," 452.

Symbolic Value, 'Exceptionalism' and Luck

Hockey collectibles are seen and treated as relics in Canada—they are, in a sense, "Canadian civil religious relics."[270] The aforementioned Lucky Loonie represents this phenomenon. Canada's Royal Mint has been "producing and distributing millions of its own Lucky Loonies for every Olympic Games since 2004."[271] In addition to being special objects to collect, Lucky Loonies allow fans to possess a token, a pseudo-religious relic that symbolizes the virtues of the players (brave, victorious) as well as their luck.[272] These shiny collectible coins symbolize the coin that has "gained fame as a lucky artifact."[273] They are at once a collectible substitute for the real coin, a symbol of memory, Canadian success, and good fortune. Canada's Mint has since expanded its hockey collectible business, and preceding the 2010 Vancouver Winter Olympics marketed and distributed a new line of "Lucky Quarters," encouraging "Canadians through television commercials to keep their eyes open for the coins during their daily transactions."[274] "Get some luck, keep the change" was the slogan—and this at once represented the value of luck, Canadian 'exceptionalism,' and possession.[275]

Proprietary Value and Self-Identity

Philosopher Meir Dan-Cohen discusses proprietary value in relation to perceptions of desire, object value, ownership value, and self-identity. Ownership is multi-dimensional. On one level: "the overall value of owning an object [is its] *proprietary value*."[276] Yet proprietary value is made up of object value (the market value of an object) and ownership value (the owner's perceived value of possessing the object).[277] On occasion, when an item (or collectible) is nearly worthless, "object value approaches the vanishing point, and proprietary value equals ownership value."[278] According to Dan-Cohen, "Although many collectibles, such as works of art, are

---

270 Bekkering, "Of "Lucky Loonies" and "Golden Pucks"," 57.
271 Ibid.
272 Ibid.
273 Ibid., 63.
274 Ibid., 66
275 Ibid.
276 Meir Dan-Cohen, "The Value of Ownership," *Global Jurist Frontiers*, 1:2 (2001): 8.
277 Ibid.
278 Ibid.

a source of gratification outside of collecting, others are not."[279] While there is a sense of value in the object itself – such as its aesthetic value or usefulness – there is also a sense of value derived from owning the object. And on occasion the gap between the value of the object and the collector's 'ownership value' can be considerable.[280] Ultimately, a collector "does not value owning these items because she values the items, but the other way around—she values the items because she owns them."[281]

Ownership is also a matter of identity, as possessing objects can act as a way of constructing and extending one's self.[282] Here, collectors might extend their identity by imagining that there is a link between "what is mine and what is me."[283] Simply put, "a conception of property as an extension of self links ownership to identity."[284] In some regards, the seeking out, gathering, and preserving of memorabilia leads collectors to construct an aspect of their self-identity. As shopping, buying, owning, and caring for items and sets of memorabilia represents a layer of the hockey collector's psyche, it is unsurprising that visitors of the HHOF "can only leave through the extensive gift shop, which seems like an exhibit itself, the souvenirs on sale include replicas of many of the Hall's memorabilia."[285] In this gift shop, which represents the culmination of a visitor's journey, people face a world of temptation where they are enticed to purchase an item and then take it home, carefully unwrap it, and either tuck it away or put it on display.

Conclusion

In this chapter I have shared a personal story about my excursion to a memorabilia show with two cousins. The experience provides details about an evening spent at a makeshift market, and it outlines key aspects of hockey collecting. What motivated my cousins and I to go to this show? What drove us to venture out one cold autumn evening, making our way through rush hour traffic and spend a few hours in a bustling room overflowing with hockey hobbyists? And what compelled me to amass a stockpile of out-of-print player guides focusing on the careers of athletes long since retired in the first place? Interspersed through my narrative vignettes I have discussed three dimensions of hockey memorabilia and

---

279 Ibid., 3.
280 Ibid
281 Ibid., 3-4.
282 Ibid.
283 Ibid., 23.
284 Ibid., 25.
285 Kidd, "The Making of a Hockey Artifact," 330.

the collector's mindset, namely: community, nostalgia, and the desire to search and own.

Collecting is "the process of actively, selectively, and passionately acquiring and possessing things removed from ordinary use and perceived as a part of a set of non-identical objects or experiences."[286] Collecting hockey memorabilia is a complex phenomenon tied to a sense of belonging to a collector community and, on a larger scale, to a national community. It can also be linked to the act of remembering, reliving, and even reimagining the past. Seeking out and gathering hockey collectibles is not only social and nostalgic, but it can also foster feelings of excitement and satisfaction associated with searching, shopping and ultimately purchasing and possessing memorabilia items. By buying different sorts of hockey artifacts, collectors feel a sense of worth, which not only ties to their notion of self-identity but also their sense of preservation.

Hockey collecting could be seen as "a materialistic luxury cost for others in the household, and represents marker goods that announce social class."[287] While this assessment is true for a great many collectors, it is not true for everyone. For some, proudly having game-used player jerseys on display in a den or living room is a marker of privilege. For others, having piles of tattered ticket stubs or stacks of old media guides is a wealth marker of a different sort. One collector could not even give away most of his hundreds of media guides when trying to de-clutter his home.[288] As hockey memorabilia indicates, there is no distinct line that separates junk from art, and collecting from hoarding. Yet hockey memorabilia is more than *useless junk*, as some might be tempted to call it. It is symbolic of the collector's – and indeed Canada's – complex notions of community, memory, ownership, identity and preservation.

---

286 Russell W. Belk, "Collecting as Luxury Consumption: Effects on Individuals and Households," *Journal of Economic Psychology,* 16 (1995): 479.

287 Carey, "Modelling Collecting Behavior," 337.

288 See Mike Beamish, "Urge to Purge Sports Collectibles 'Treasures' a Tidy Process," *Vancouver Sun*, May 11 2015. Accessed July 15, 2015. http://www.vancouversun.com/life/Urge+purge+sports+collectibles+treasures+tidy+process/11045212/story.html

CONCLUSION:
Admit One

People access hockey in many different ways, from many different places, as the varied chapters in this book illustrate. The fans, players,
coaches, community and parents in this book each find their own unique
way 'in' to the game. For some, the way into the game is through a nation's
shared history of a sport or a team. For others working around the ice, it
is an activist's way of beating the class system. For coaches, staff, parents
and others, it is a contribution towards developing and supporting some of
the world's most elite athletes. Let us summarize the six portals to hockey
described in *Next to the Ice*.

Cam's cosmology, a history of hockey, describes the Great Man theory of
history, the archetype used by so many historians and politicians, including former Prime Minister Stephen Harper, Stan and Shirley Fischler in
their *Heroes and Hockey: Voices from NHL's Past!*, and Lord Stanley himself.
Where this concept of the 'great man' came from is also touched upon in
Kara's 'yellow brick road' and Christopher's debate on masculinity. Kara's chapter points out that hockey evolved as Canada's sport through its
aristocratic beginnings on the lawns of Lord Stanley's Rideau Hall, Queen
Victoria's representative in Canada; McGill University's elite clubs; and
the Lord council's best friend, John A. MacDonald. For nationalists, this
early history of the country and the sport is what draws them to the game.
The nation's history is the entry point to hockey for historians and fans.

Christopher's exploration of men and masculinities pulls this thread
deeper through the layers of hockey's place in our past. What makes a
man 'masculine'? How is one 'great' through sport? Perhaps one is ex-

pected to perpetuate strength (pp. 28-29), even through accepted physical injury, to receive those patriarchal rewards described in Cam and Kara's chapters on that shared history by the ice. Hockey clubs stereotyped young athletes from lower socio-economic backgrounds as 'fighters' because of their class status; however, for those athletes, professional hockey was a job and a way out, and it became the local community's view, the fans of *their* players, of a way to 'beat the system.' Fighting in hockey, for fans, meant hope. It was a way of voices being heard. A way to legitimately fight the upper class. The sport became a microcosm of society's own class issues and stereotypes, and for those activists pushing the definition of 'the great man,' it was the last barrier to be broken. Hockey was a door for enforcers, for activists, for fans wanting to see change. Nowhere was this more evident than with the recent fan promotion and support of player-enforcer John Scott in the 2016 NHL All-Star game. This story is but a nucleus of the continuing fight of fans against the powers and the equity of the hockey 'aristocracy.' Fans as activists of social justice and power find their way into hockey through issues of masculinity, fighting, and cultural recognition.

And for all three of the authors here, the door to hockey remains one of a mutual connection. Cam is a hockey collector and fan; Christopher a coach and former player; and Kara, a parent. The only link between the three is hockey. Parts of this book you are reading were written right beside the ice. And the debates and issues and discussions within this book take place every single day in arenas across the country, perhaps not in such detail, but they are discussed by each connection. For example, what fan or coach or parent or player has not had a conversation about the 'organization' and what it is doing wrong? Who hasn't had a debate about a hit or penalty call? Who hasn't spent hours wandering the stalls at tournaments or games to view the merchandise and collectibles? What person *next to the ice* has not seen or held or owned a hockey card? And who has not marveled at the abilities of a lean, exceptional 200-pound athlete on skates and ice with a stick? This is what we share as authors and readers. And whether the 'great man,' the historical tie, the struggle for equity or notoriety or voice, or the pride in developing the world's best athletes, is our way in - we are in. We are there. *We are next to the ice.*

SELECTED WORKS

Adams, Mary Louise. *Artistic Impressions: Figure Skating, Masculinity, and the Limits of Sport.* Toronto, ON: University of Toronto Press, 2011.

Allain, Kristi A. "'Real Fast and Tough': The Construction of Canadian Hockey Masculinity." *Sociology of Sport Journal, 25 (2008)*: 462-481.

Appy, Christian G. *Working-Class War: American Combat Soldiers & Vietnam.* Chapel Hill, NC: The University of North Carolina Press, 1993.

Branch, John. *Boy on Ice: The Life and Death of Derek Boogaard.* Toronto, ON: Harper Collins Publishers Ltd., 2014.

Stephen Brunt. *Gretzky's Tears: Hockey, Canada, and the Day Everything Changed.* Toronto, ON: Knoph Canada, 2009.

Buma, Michael. *Refereeing Identity: The Cultural Work of Canadian Hockey Novels.* Kingston, ON: McGill-Queen's Press, 2015.

Blake, Jason. *Canadian Hockey Literature: A Thematic Study.* Toronto, ON: University of Toronto Press, 2010.

Bowlsby, Craig H. *1913: The Year They Invented the Future of Hockey.* Vancouver, BC: Knights of Winter, 2013.

Campbell, Ken with Jim Parcels. *Selling the Dream: How Hockey Parents and Their Kids Are Paying the Price for Our National Obsession.* Toronto, ON: Viking Press, 2013.

Chuvalo, George with Murray Greig. *Chuvalo: A Fighter's Life.* Toronto, ON: HarperCollins, 2013.

Cole, Stephen. *Hockey Night Fever: Mullets, Mayhem and the Game's Coming of Age in the 1970s.* Toronto, ON: Doubleday, 2015.

Dryden, Ken, and Roy MacGregor. *Home Game: Hockey and Life in Canada.* Toronto, ON: McClelland & Stewart, 1990.

Fischler, Stan, and Shirley Fischler. *Heroes and History: Voices from the NHL's Past!* Toronto, ON: McGraw-Hill Ryerson, 1994.

Fleury, Theo with Kristie McLellan Day. *Playing With Fire: The Highest Highs and The Lowest Lows of Theo Fleury.* Toronto, ON: HarperCollins Publishers, 2011.

Fosty, George, and Darril Fosty. *Black Ice: The Lost History of the Colored Hockey League of the Maritimes, 1895-1925.* New York, NY: Stryker-Indigo Publishing Company, 2004.

Goyens, Chrys, and Allan Turoweitz. *Lions in Winter (revised second edition).* Toronto, ON: McGraw-Hill Ryerson, 1994.

Greig, Christopher J., and Wayne Martino. *Canadian Men and Masculinities: Historical and Contemporary Perspectives.* Toronto, ON: Canadian Scholars' Press, 2013.

Gretzky, Walter. *On Family, Hockey and Healing.* Toronto, ON: Random House, 2001.

Harper, Stephen J. *A Great Game: The Forgotten Leafs and the Rise of Professional Hockey*. Toronto, ON: Simon & Schuster, 2013.

Holzman, Morey, and Joseph Nieforth. *Deceptions and Doublecross: How the NHL Conquered Hockey*. Toronto, ON: The Dundurn Group, 2002.

James, Valmore with John Gallagher. *Black Ice: The Val James Story*. Toronto, ON: ECWPress, 2015.

Jenish, D'Arcy. *The NHL: 100 Years of On-Ice Action and Boardroom Battles*. Toronto, ON: Doubleday Canada, 2013.

Kennedy, Sheldon with James Grainger. *Why I Didn't Say Anything*. London, ON: Insomniac Press, 2011.

Kitchen, Paul. *Win, Tie, or Wrangle: The Inside Story of the Old Ottawa Senators 1883-1935*. Newcastle, ON: Penumbria Press, 2008.

Laraque, Georges with Pierre Thibeault. *Georges Laraque: The Story of the NHL's Unlikeliest Tough Guy*. Toronto, ON: Viking Canada, 2011.

Leach, Reggie. *The Riverton Rifle: My Story-Straight Shooting on Hockey and on Life*. Vancouver, BC: Greystone Books, 2015.

Liebling, A. J. *A Neutral Corner: Boxing Essays*. New York, NY: Farrar, Straus and Giroux, 1990.

Feldman, Doug. *Keith Magnuson: The Inspiring Life and Times of a Beloved Blackhawk*. Chicago, IL: Triumph Books, 2013.

Marks, Don. *They Call Me Chief: Warriors on Ice*. Winnipeg, MB: J. Gordon Shillingford Publishing, 2008.

McAllister, Ron. *Hockey Heroes: Canadian Sports Album*. Toronto, ON: McClelland & Stewart Limited, 1949.

McFarlane, Brian. *50 Years of Hockey: An Intimate History of the National Hockey League*. Toronto, ON: Pagurian Press Limited, 1967.

McFarlane, Brian. *Proud Past, Bright Future: One Hundred Years of Canadian Women's Hockey*. Toronto, ON: Stoddart, 1995.

McKenzie, Bob. *Hockey Confidential: Inside Stories from People Inside the Game*. Toronto, ON: Harper Collins Publisher Ltd., 2014.

McKinley, Michael. *Hockey: A People's History*. Toronto, ON: McClelland & Stewart, 2006.

Orwell, George. *Essays*. New York, NY: Alfred A. Knopf, 2002.

Pronger, Brian. *The Arena of Masculinity: Sports, Homosexuality and the Meaning of Sex*. Toronto, ON: University of Toronto Press, 1992.

Quarrington, Paul (editor). *Original Six: True Stories from Hockey's Classic Era*. Toronto, ON: Reed Books Canada, 1996.

Reid, Ken. *Hockey Card Stories: True Tales from Your Favourite Players*. Toronto, ON: ECW Press, 2014.

Robinson, Laura. *Crossing The Line: Violence and Sexual Assault in Canada's National Sport*. Toronto, ON: McClelland & Stewart, 1998.

Ronberg, Gary. *The Violent Game: Close Look at Pro Hockey and Its Bad Guys*. Englewood Cliffs, NJ: Prentice Hall, 1965.

Roxborough, Henry Hall. *The Stanley Cup Story*. Toronto, ON: McGraw-Hill Limited Toronto, 1964.

Roy, Michel. *Patrick Roy: Winning. Nothing Else*. Mississauga, ON: John Wiley & Sons Canada, Ltd., 2007.

Sanderson, Derek with Kevin Shea. *Crossing The Line: The Outrageous Story of a Hockey Original*. Toronto, ON: HarperCollins, 2012.

Shultz, Dave with Stan Fischler. *The Hammer: Confessions of a Hockey Enforcer*. New York, NY: Summit Books, 1980.

Tufts, Allyson. *Lessons from Behind the Glass: The Journey of a Hockey Mom*. (Self-published) Ottawa, 2016.

Valliant, Paul M. *Minor Hockey to NHL: Parents' Survival Guide*. Victoria, BC: Trafford Publishing, 2007.

Whitehead, Eric. *Cyclone Taylor: A Hockey Legend*. Toronto, ON: Doubleday Canada Limited, 1977.

Whitehead, Eric. *The Patricks: Hockey's Royal Family*. Toronto, ON: Doubleday Canada Limited, 1980.

Williams, Dave, with James Lawton. *Tiger: A Hockey Story*. Toronto, ON: Douglas & McIntyre, 1984.

Wong, John. *Lords of the Rinks: The Emergence of the National Hockey League 1875-1936*. Toronto, ON: University of Toronto Press, 2005.

INDEX

Y

Z

ABOUT THE AUTHORS

Cam Cobb is a professor at the University of Windsor. He researches social justice, special education, and adult learning. Cobb's work has been published in the *British Journal of Special Education, the International Journal of Inclusive Education, Per la filosofia, and Cinema: Philosophy and the Moving Image.* He is an avid collector of the 'Jim Proudfoot player guidebooks.'

Christopher J. Greig is a professor at the University of Windsor in Education and Women's and Gender Studies. A historian of gender, Greig researches Canadian men, boys, and masculinities. His research has been published in *Educational Review,* the *Brock Journal of Education,* and the *Alberta Journal of Educational Research.* Greig is the co-editor of *Canadian Men and Masculinities* (2012) and author of *Ontario Boys: Masculinity and the Idealized Boyhood in Postwar Ontario* (2014). Greig's life-long interest in ice hockey started in the winter of 1969, at the age of four, when his father, Ted, built a back yard rink in London, Ontario.

Kara Smith is editor of Teaching, Learning Assessing (Mosaic Press, 2007) and the author of *The Mâlain-Chatham Diaries* (2015). She is an award-winning education professor; international writer-in-residence; former national player; and a frequent contributor to hockey parent culture and psychological development in Ontario.